Books by Elizabeth Post

Emily Post's Book of Etiquette, 12th Edition
Emily Post's Book of Etiquette for Young People
The Wonderful World of Weddings
Please, Say Please

Please, Say Please

Please, Say Please

A Common Sense Guide to Bringing Up Your Child

Elizabeth L. Post

EMILY POST INSTITUTE, INC.

Little, Brown and Company—Boston—Toronto

FIRST EDITION

T 08/72

Library of Congress Cataloging in Publication Data

Post, Elizabeth L
    Please, say please.

    1. Children--Management.   2. Etiquette for children
and youth.   I.   Title.
˙HQ769.P824   649'.1   72-690
ISBN 0-316-714658

*Published simultaneously in Canada
by Little, Brown & Company (Canada) Limited*

PRINTED IN THE UNITED STATES OF AMERICA

To my greatest inspirations
and severest critics —

Allen, Bill, Cindy, and Peter

Contents

Introduction

Young parents today realistically wonder: "Are manners important anymore? Is 'etiquette' outdated or hypocritical?"

These are sensible, honest questions and they may even be carried one step further — "Do manners, and etiquette, as we think of them, still exist at all?"

They not only exist, they are just as rigidly adhered to today as they were in your great-grandmother's time. The catch is that they are totally different. And they *should* be different, because our life is so very different from hers. In the Victorian age, there was a tremendous emphasis on personal privacy. People did not *want* intimacy and any effort to force it was considered boorish and unwelcome. Etiquette decreed that only the most intimate family and friends called each other by their first names, and it was carried so far that many wives never dared speak to their husbands by other than "Mr. Bradshaw." Greetings and introductions reflected the reserve. The "May I present . . ." and "How do you do?" allowed very little opening for new acquaintances to get close to each other. If anyone overstepped the bounds, he was frowned upon and ostracized — as uncouth, pushy, and *not* a gentleman.

Today, our outlook — and consequently our manners — is totally changed. The emphasis is exactly the reverse — we admire informality, we look up to ease of manners, naturalness, and friendliness. But what are accepted as good manners are as rigidly enforced as were the Victorian rules. We would frown on, just as severely, and ostracize just as quickly, the person who *refused* to exchange first names when introduced, or to respond to our efforts to be friendly even without an introduction. What is right for the times and the ambient becomes part of etiquette, and becomes so natural that those who behave according to the accepted standards are not even conscious that they are doing so. Most manners evolve of their own accord, and the best ones survive and are acted upon until the life-style changes so much, again, that they become obsolete.

The answer to those questions lies in an understanding of the real meaning of etiquette and manners. While the word "consideration" doesn't cover all of the aspects of etiquette, perhaps it is the closest synonym.

Good manners are based on thoughtfulness for others, and their primary aim is to make human relationships as smooth and as pleasant as possible. Furthermore, the person whose manners are natural and unpretentious is an attractive person, and blessed with self-confidence and self-respect.

So, when someone asks, "Are manners important?" I can honestly answer, "Of course they are." Surely, wanting one's child to be a considerate, attractive, self-respecting person is a normal desire, and giving him a knowledge of manners is a giant step toward that goal. Without the patient, continuous instruction and example set by one generation for the next, all the experience of civilization through the ages would be lost. This would be a true tragedy because among the thousands of rules — the contradictory, the changing, the useless, and the exaggerated — there are hundreds of real value. It is your job to sort out and pass on the best. By making those an integral part of your child's personality, and by giving him the prerogative of discarding, adding, and changing them as his experience grows, you will help him to grow up popular, at ease, and with manners appropriate to his time.

There is another, rather less noble reason for stressing manners. In fact, it is purely selfish, but it is very human. We want our children to be admired not only for their own sakes, but as a reflection on us. I'm sure you have seen the look on a mother's face when someone says to her, "Your Sally is so well behaved." You've also undoubtedly seen the blushing mother who has been asked to take her little boy out of the store because he is annoying the customers!

Pride in your child is a perfectly natural — and desirable — emotion. Unless you are very unusual parents, you are going to get a tremendous kick out of his accomplishments. You will never forget the moment when he says his first word, or the first time he takes three steps without falling down. There's no feeling in the world like it. For your pleasure and success as a parent, never lose this sense of excitement. Too many parents allow themselves to get bored with their children or they let the inevitable irritations override the pleasures of bringing up a family. If you realize that these "firsts" — some small, some large — will continue as long as your child is growing up, you also must realize that this will be an unending source of excitement and satisfaction.

Many of you are afraid that you will feel confined by the necessity of staying with your children constantly. That feeling, unfortunately, breeds resentment. You may think that your skills are being wasted and you are not making the contribution to society of which you are capable. Actually, if you keep your values in perspective, you will realize that, in bringing up children who are considerate, who are able to think for themselves, and who have a sense of responsibility, you are making a very real contribution to society. You are quite justified in not wishing to spend all your life in domestic surroundings, but during the first months of your child's life, your primary interest must revolve around him. Once his feeling of security, and his confidence in his place in the world, are established, you may, without risking his stability, turn to a career.

Aside from the damage you could do your baby by not devoting enough attention to him in his early months, you would be depriving yourself of a unique and fascinating experience. Raising a child can be great fun and one of the most rewarding occupations in the world. To enjoy it to the full you must regard it as a welcome challenge, and to come through it unscathed, you must have a sense of humor. Because children are people, and people are not perfect. You might just as well throw out any preconceived picture you have of yourself smilingly rocking an immaculate, cooing baby to sleep in a sun-filled, spotless nursery. You might find that picture on the cover of a woman's magazine, but you will never find it in real life.

Because growing up is part of life, and life is a

hodgepodge — trial and error, success and failure, and sorrow and joy. Part of life is the seamy side — dirt, ugliness, and violence — and part is beauty and goodness. You cannot isolate a child from the seamy side — nor should you. You *can* prepare him to cope with it by teaching him to meet it face to face, and by helping him to discriminate between the good and the bad.

Let's assume that you accept the fact that manners, at least those based on consideration and practicality, *are* important. The next question follows naturally: "How do I go about teaching my child good manners?" To answer, "By patient, constant instruction, and example" is perfectly correct, but it is a gross oversimplification that does not take into consideration the tremendous diversity among children — and mothers — or the emotional aspects of rearing children. Some parents are capable of considerable emotional detachment; the feelings of others are so involved that they cannot make a gesture which is not dictated by too much love, too much anger, or too much fear. One set of parents may deprive their child of the affection and warmth he needs, but another set will cripple him more with extremes of overindulgence and punishment. Some unrestrained emotion is necessary to every child, but so are periods of calm, during which he can relax, rest, and have time to absorb what is happening to him.

The need for parents to exercise restraint — to keep emotions under control, and to face situations coolly, with common sense and a sense of humor — is of prime importance. So many young mothers who face every sort of problem — financial, social, and so on — with intelligence and equanimity, fall apart completely when their child has an emotional or behavior problem. This is, of course, because they let their emotions overcome their reason. If they could only consider the problem from the third-person viewpoint, their everyday intelligence would assert itself, and common sense would prevail.

These are generalizations and somewhat abstract thoughts — this book is actually devoted to giving you more down-to-earth suggestions for teaching manners. But it is concerned with the *which* and the *why*, as well as the *how*.

Almost all young couples live very informally today, and therefore the old "rules" are less rigid. We do not worry much about which side of the plate the used napkin goes on, or whether or not one finishes every morsel on that plate. These questions simply do not seem terribly important anymore, and whatever you do about them will surely not hurt anyone else. But in other areas there are still right ways and wrong ways, and they are generally the areas in which we touch other peoples' lives. Those manners *are* important. Showing respect for older people by standing for them, holding a door or carrying a heavy package for a woman, rules of introductions which help to avoid embarrassment, are all things that children should be taught. Let them make a choice later about which rules they wish to observe, but if they are not exposed to a substantial number as they grow up, they will have little to compare to, and nothing on which to base, their own standards. If you *expose* your children to all the rules you think worthwhile, and *insist* that they observe the ones which are most important, the next generation will have a jumping-off place.

You may not remember it now but your parents undoubtedly tried to give you a jumping-off place too. They probably made mistakes — you will too. However, I am sure they did their best to give you what they thought you wanted and needed, and to teach you the standards and values that seemed important to them. Some members of our generation are distressed by the results of our own efforts — others, including myself, are proud. In any case *you* are the result, just as your children will be the fruition of your efforts. I truly hope that you will profit and learn from our experiences, because — now it is your turn.

You will notice as you read this book, that except in specific instances, I refer to "the child" or "your child" as "he." This does not mean that the material is intended only for boys. It is a matter of simplifying the writing. It would be most awkward and impractical to continually say "he or she," "his or hers," and so on. When the subject of the section is particularly feminine, curtsying or playing with dolls for example, I have used girls' names or used the word "she." In all other cases, please assume that the information applies to children of both sexes.

I

Who Is My Baby?

Wʜᴏ — ᴀɴᴅ ᴡʜᴀᴛ — ɪꜱ ᴍʏ ʙᴀʙʏ? Who are we — his parents? What do we want for him? How can we best help him in growing up?

These are questions which all parents should start to think about before their baby is born, and they must continue to ask them, and to reappraise them, as he develops.

There are as many answers as there are mothers with babies. We certainly do not all want the same things for our children, nor do we wish to achieve what we want in the same ways. The answers to these questions merely provide foundations for *your* attitude toward *your* baby, which will serve you as guidelines in all situations. As soon as you decide *what* you want his life to mean to him and *how* you can help him to find that meaning, half the battle is won. To have a "plan of attack," a preconsidered route to follow, will make rearing your child a great deal easier.

I cannot give you all the answers that are right for

you and your child. I can, and I will, suggest an attitude and a course of action, both of which are based on mutual respect, common sense, and love.

"Who is my baby?"

He is, of course, basically a product of the union between you and your husband. But he is much more than that. He is a person in his own right. He has his own personality, his own physical characteristics, and his own capacity for development. He is not an unresponsive "object," he is not a possession. He is a member of a family and his presence will inevitably affect the life of that family, just as the existence of parents, brothers, and sisters will influence him. From the day he is born his mere presence will to some extent alter the habits and the personalities of those around him. No matter how small, he is a being to be concerned about and reckoned with.

For example, the arrival of the first baby creates an enormous change in the "free" life a young couple has been living. It will also have a drastic effect on the relationship between husband and wife. Until a child arrives, the woman's love and affection were her husband's alone. Suddenly, his freedom is curtailed, and his wife's interests necessarily are divided between him and the baby. The danger is that too *much* of her time and love will be devoted to the baby, and that is no better for the child than it is for her husband. The baby must be made to realize he is a welcome addition to an already-established family. The relationships were there — they were not created simply for his benefit. A baby does, of course, require a great portion of a mother's time and effort, but he will receive that during the day when she is alone with him. When her husband is at home, it is in the best interests of both father and child to put the husband's comfort and needs first. He will have far more interest in the baby if he does not feel the new arrival has supplanted him in his wife's affection, and his own love for the child will be strengthened when he knows he has not "lost" his wife to the baby.

Similarly, the birth of a second baby has an inevitable effect on an older child. A two-year-old who has been the sole target of parental love since the day he was born is not going to willingly share that place with a new brother or sister. I will go into this relationship in more detail in Chapter 8, but the point to be made here is that a mother must not cheat the older child of the attention that is due him by letting the household revolve around the baby, any more than

5

she should deprive her husband of his full share of affection. In short, one facet of the answer to "Who is my baby?" is that he is a part — a very important part — of the family, but he is not the center of it.

In the very beginning the baby's potential is, of course, totally undeveloped. But within him lies an enormous capacity to learn and to develop. From the moment he can focus his eyes, he will constantly be changed by what he sees around him. With each physical advance he will expand mentally more rapidly. His personality will change from time to time and he will go through a variety of stages. He may start out by being a docile, quiet baby and develop into a holy terror when he learns to walk. Or he may be a seemingly well-adjusted, happy two-year-old who becomes sullen and unresponsive at four. Your reactions to him and your attitude toward him must change too, if you are to help him through these steps. You must never lose sight of the fact that one part or another of his personality is developing at each new level, and it is your job to encourage the growth of the desirable traits, and discourage the bad.

Too many parents think of their child — especially a very small child — as a member of an alien race. They assume that, simply because he is inarticulate, he cannot understand or communicate, much like a foreigner who does not speak English. They do not give him an opportunity to show what he can do. They continually underestimate his abilities and therefore make martyrs of themselves by giving him too constant care and endless attention. They underestimate the child's intelligence — speaking *about* him as if he were not there and speaking *to* him in baby talk — as if he could not understand ordinary words. These parents are failing the child and themselves. They are strangling his development and they are depriving themselves of the pleasure of seeing his personality emerge.

"Who is my baby?" He is, then, a small body, with good and bad potentials. He is ready and able to learn, to assimilate, to grow, and to emerge an adult. He is something to be nurtured and cherished, but not possessed. Although he is part of you, and his father, he is not either or both. He is his *own* person, a human being, to be liked or disliked, scorned or admired, accepted or rejected, for himself alone.

"Who are we — his parents?"

You are the people to whom he will turn for love, for solace, for physical care, for advice and for understanding. You and your husband are his source of security. You are providers, for both his bodily and his emotional needs. During his early years at least, you will also be responsible for his discipline. And, perhaps most important of all, you are his teachers. You and your husband will set the example which he will follow.

While you are disciplining, nurturing, and teaching you will also be reaping tremendous rewards. Each accomplishment — physical or mental — is a source of pride and joy. The day the baby chomps on your finger and you shriek, "He's got a TOOTH!" is only the beginning. The next week, the next month, the next year will continue to provide excitement if you keep looking for it. How delighted the father must have been when his seven-year-old son brought home this composition: "Fathers are neat. They are there when you want them."

What are the qualifications for a successful parent? There are many, of course, but there are four basic characteristics without which it would be very difficult to raise your baby successfully. They are integrity, common sense, tolerance, and a sense of humor.

The extent to which a child relies on his parents' integrity is frightening. Deliberately or carelessly destroying that faith can have a devastating effect on his sense of security and his respect for you. If you encourage your youngster — as you should — to depend on your word and to trust you implicitly, and then he finds out that your word is *not* dependable, you will deprive him of the most important source of security he has. No matter how difficult it may be for you, *never* tell your child a lie. Even when he is a mere toddler, don't answer his questions with a "yes" or "no" unless "yes" or "no" is entirely true. If it is only partially so, explain the conditions. For example, when your three-year-old asks, "Did the stork really bring me to you in the hospital, Mommy?" don't take the easy way out and say, "Of course." At that age he does not need to learn the facts of life, but you can satisfy his curiosity easily and honestly, "You *did* come to me in the hospital, Terry, but a stork didn't bring you. You were such a nice big baby a stork couldn't have carried you, so Dr. Jones brought you to me instead." If you do not know the answer, say so, but don't lie your way out of it. If you have a valid reason for not wanting to answer his question, tell him that, too. But be sure your reason *is* valid. An evasion such as "because you're too young to understand," can only hamper your child's curiosity and the development of his intelligence.

Common sense enables one to meet everyday crises

9

without panic and to solve problems by using intelligence and experience. It acts as a restraint. It will keep you from becoming hysterical over minor problems, and help you to try to work them out yourself, rather than making unnecessary demands on others, or upsetting your child by exaggerated concern. The mother who goes into a panic at the first sign of a sniffle or the slightest scratch on her child's knee, and calls the doctor demanding instant help, has gone off half-cocked. By using common sense, and stopping to see if she could not take care of the problem herself, the hysterical mother would save the doctor's time, save her money, and save herself from making a mountain out of a molehill.

If she only panics on rare occasions when circumstances have combined to make her so up-tight that she cannot control herself, little harm will be done. But most people who panic easily, panic often, and it can become a damaging pattern of behavior for mother *and* child. The youngster whose mother goes into hysterics when he gets the slightest cut or bump is soon going to become a sissy, a hypochondriac, or totally self-centered. His mother is failing to teach him that no one can get through life without a few bruises, and to instill in him a little stoicism. Surely the child who sees a balanced approach to childhood mishaps is better prepared for serious ones later.

Without tolerance, a parent could not face the disappointments that rearing a child is bound to bring at times. It is the trait which allows you to bridge the "generation gap" and to see your child's side of the question. When your daughter declares she hates dolls, and you had been hoping for a very feminine, domestically inclined little girl, after three rambunctious boys, or your son says he doesn't want to take tennis lessons because he would rather collect butterflies, it is tolerance which allows you to say, "Fine, let's concentrate on *your* interest — what's right for *you*." Parents who are tolerant of their children's shortcomings are usually quick to recognize their own. They know that teaching one thing and practicing another is a waste of time, and they are as stern or sterner about their own slips than those of their children.

Tolerance also helps you to expect and accept your youngster's mistakes. He will make them — we all do. In fact, if he didn't make mistakes, he would have little to learn and you would have little to teach. Knowing this, you should be tolerant of his shortcomings and ready to laugh at them. It may be hard to keep your temper when your preschooler says loudly,

"Mommy, isn't that the lady you said always wears the funniest-looking hats?" but tolerance and a sense of humor will see you through. You may have temporarily lost a friend, but not if she has a sense of humor too! In any case, you have been given a wonderful opening to teach your youngster a lesson about consideration, and not hurting other people's feelings.

Parents who have a well-developed sense of humor, also have an unerring sense of proportion. Neither the shortcomings nor the achievements of their children are given too much importance. Misdeeds are taken seriously, but not as a calamity, and very often it is the ability to see the funny side which makes this possible. A parent's sense of humor can help to prevent the child or his actions from becoming too "special." Your youngster must know at all times that you are *with* him, but not to the exclusion of other people and interests.

Most young parents aim too high — they want to be the "perfect" parents. I would like to emphasize right here that it is neither possible nor desirable to be a "perfect" parent. To train your child successfully, you must impose a strenuous course of self-discipline on yourself, or you will not be able to maintain the standards you set. You still will not achieve "perfection" but you will have done the best that you can —

according to your ability. Complete perfection would be impossible to live with, in any case. Your child is not looking for an ideal — a god — to live with, he is looking for a warm human being, and just how admirable can any human being be? No one has ever lived who did not occasionally display impatience, annoyance, or misunderstanding. To your youngster's sharp eyes, the flaws in your character are very visible. It would be unrealistic — and lacking in honesty — to deny their existence. There is one quality which children admire enormously in their parents — honesty in their appraisal of themselves, the ability to admit their faults. Your child will truly appreciate your honesty about what you *are*, as well as what you would like to be. Shortcomings are human, in many instances even appealing, and the parent who is admittedly less than perfect makes a far more desirable companion than one whose perfection makes him inhuman, and unattainable. The mother (or father) who denies her own shortcomings, or pretends to be something she is not, will soon have little influence on her child. The smallest toddler's perception is very keen. Even when his judgment is misled by familiarity and misplaced confidence a child's ability to see through you can be recognized in his steady, questioning gaze.

Furthermore, perfection implies a static condition,

and bringing up a child is a constantly changing oper-
ation. What is "perfect" in a three-year-old, or in his
parents' attitude toward him, is not necessarily perfect
at all in a six-year-old. Perfection must change according to the circumstances — one should not look for a
finished product, but for a growing, developing situation. Striving for perfection is a self-defeating task —
don't try. Do the best you can and satisfy yourself that
it *is* the best for that particular moment, but accept
the fact that by tomorrow you will have to meet a new
criterion.

If you and your husband can view your child impartially enough, you will learn a tremendous amount
from him. Not, of course, as much as he will learn,
because he has so much farther to go, but enough to
enrich your lives and broaden your viewpoints greatly.
By observing his patience, or lack of it, his stubbornness or flexibility, his independence or reliance on you,
you who are encouraging or discouraging these traits
can apply the same disciplines to yourself.

When a child grows up in a home where consideration of others, unselfishness, and gracious behavior are
taken for granted, these characteristics will probably
become part of his nature, even though they may man-
ifest themselves differently from the parents' behavior.
He must be instructed patiently, reminded constantly,

and encouraged to observe from the time he can understand, but all the reminding, observing, or teaching in the world will do no good if the example is not there to follow. Children are in part what their environment makes of them, and it is up to you as a parent to create the proper environment.

There used to be, and still are, a number of jokes and snide remarks about manners, usually with reference especially to the manners of the wealthy. "The newly rich have more comforts, but the newly poor have more manners," is an anonymous example. Henry James wrote, "There are bad manners everywhere, but an aristocracy is bad manners organized." Frankly, these implied criticisms of manners are quite justified when they refer, as they were intended to do, to the la-di-da manners of Little Lord Fauntleroy. But those mannerisms and affectations are not what count today. What *is* important is good, solid, decent consideration of others, and that is available to everyone — rich and poor alike. Poverty and illiteracy are handicaps, to be sure, but our country is filled with men who have risen to the top of their professions, triumphing over both. And there are many other mothers and fathers from the simplest backgrounds who have created homes where an atmosphere of security, confidence, trust, and love satisfies, nurtures, and influences their children throughout their lives. Self-control, integrity, patience, kindness, tolerance, and common sense are qualities which know no distinction as to wealth or poverty. They are as common among the poor as the rich. And no matter who you are, or what your background, it is impossible for you to teach your youngster truth, fairness, loyalty, and consideration if you do not possess those qualities yourself.

One must be very careful in setting an example for children, because there are some traits which seem to be desirable in a parent which in truth may have a detrimental effect. The unselfish mother who gives unstintingly to her child may end up with a very selfish child because everything has been given to him and he has never had to share. Here, again, is she being honest in her reasons for giving unstintingly? Is she truly thinking of what is best for the child, or is she satisfying her own image of herself as an unselfish person? The strong-minded father who smooths every path for his son may end up with a weakling — the boy never learns to make any effort for himself. One of the greatest handicaps you can give a child is to do too much for him. He must learn — to the best of his ability at each stage of his development — the truth of the saying "God helps those that help themselves."

One would assume that to be a good parent, a

mother or father must have unqualified love for a child. It is true that love for your child is the first and most important requirement, but the emotion of love alone is not enough. Love is the most beautiful of all human emotions, but to be enduring it must be blended with friendship, discipline, and sense as well as sentiment.

To think that your child is perfect in every way, to be blind to the inevitable flaws he must have, is not proof that you love — it is merely proof that you lack good sense. If, in his preschool years, you give him nothing but unwarranted praise and unquestioning devotion, he will develop a very inflated sense of his own importance. As he begins to leave the home and is thrown in with playmates, schoolmates, and other outsiders, he will be rapidly deflated when he finds that their world does not revolve around him. This is a far harder way to learn than had love been tempered with common sense at home!

The overcritical parent who constantly nags and belittles every effort his youngster makes does just as much harm. He may believe that he is giving evidence of his love by striving to make his child even more perfect, but the result is more likely a defeatist attitude and a total lack of self-confidence and respect. How many children have failed miserably in school or become dropouts because their parents, under the aura of "love," have expected too much, and pushed too hard?

If the love that develops between you and your baby is a *rational* love, you will avoid the pitfalls that many parents encounter when their child passes the toddler stage — when his reactions stop being purely emotional, and he begins to think. If you have encouraged him to see and recognize your faults as well as your virtues — and if you have accepted his — your relationship will not be in much danger of a real crisis when he reaches the "questioning" age. One of the most common disasters of the teen years occurs when a youngster finds that the parent he thought of as the epitome of virtue and dependability — is not. The idol is smashed and the reaction is often one of anger and rebellion. This is easily avoided if you have convinced him all along that no idol is perfect or unbreakable, and that unshakable love accepts the bad along with the good.

What, then, is perfect love? It is a combination of emotion and rationality. It is also devotion, friendship, understanding, restraint, tolerance, admiration, and respect. It is love that permits a child to share it and feel its presence and support without being stifled or overcome. And above all, it is unquestioning and unquestioned — it is love that, no matter how trying the circumstances, is *always there.*

It is an old saw that parents must *never* undermine each other. They may disagree in private about a decision one or the other has rendered, but they never fail to back that decision up in front of their child. Unfortunately, a great many parents do not realize this, and the result is, at first, confusion, and later, total lack of discipline. Just because this has not been said time and time again doesn't mean that it is not still true — and important.

When Johnny is three or four he is constantly subjected to his mother and father's differences of opinion about his upbringing. His mother has told him he may watch one last cartoon at 6:00 and then he will go to bed. At 6:10 his father comes home and upsets the decision. "Oh, Jane, let him stay up another half hour — it won't hurt him." In the beginning Johnny isn't seriously harmed by an occasional "treat" like this, but his father continually contradicts his mother's words about what he must eat, when he may go out to play, where he may go, and so on. Gradually Johnny realizes that if he can pit Mother's authority against Daddy's, by delaying decisions until Daddy comes home, he will almost always come out on top. Aside from the antagonism between his parents, the atmosphere in the home is one of confusion and total lack of respect for authority.

Every young couple should discuss and come to an agreement about this while their first child is still in the bassinet. Mother is going to have to "lay down the law" as best she can while father is at work, and they cannot foresee in advance every situation which will arise. But parents should, insofar as possible, agree on their overall approach to discipline and then carry it out, whether together or separately. Then no matter if father agrees with mother's decision or not, he must support her in that instance.

A parent usually falls into this trap because of a hidden desire to win the child's affection away from the other parent. It is more apt to be a fault on the part of the man, because he is away all day and may feel jealous of the closeness developing between his wife and his children. It may even work — for the moment — but in the long run it inevitably leads not to love or admiration, but to scorn and disrespect. This disrespect is not only directed at the offending parent, but at both. Reversing a decision in this way is really just a form of "bribery," and even a very small youngster will soon lose any admiration he may have for an adult who must resort to bribes to win his affection.

If you find yourselves contradicting each other in front of your child, or if you have constant disagreements about how to handle him, sit down together and examine your motives. You will, very probably, find that you are competing for the youngster's affection or attention. To face this honestly — and admit it — is very difficult to do, but it will be worth the anguish for you as parents — and it is essential for the good of the child.

"What do we want for our baby, and how can we help him to grow up?"

In nine cases out of ten, I am sure that people who were asked the first part of the question above would answer, "Happiness." But life really has a great deal more to offer than happiness. We surely want satisfaction and contentment for our children too, which though related, are not synonymous with happiness. And to make one appreciate happiness we would have to wish for occasional trouble to be faced, or setbacks to be overcome.

A challenge may not add to one's happiness but the meeting of it can add greatly to one's satisfaction. Our children will not experience the best in life if they do not face challenges — whether personal ones such as getting through school, or working for a cause they believe in.

There is a distinction, too, between happiness and contentment. Happiness is more applicable as a goal for the young. It is more emotional, often more fleeting, and something to fight for. Contentment comes later in life when one no longer wishes to fight. It is more passive, less stimulating, but in its own way as rewarding. We would certainly want our children eventually to achieve contentment. To do so, it is almost essential that they also know the *satisfaction* of having gotten the most that they could out of their lives, and having done the best that they could with the opportunities they had.

Prospective parents, or parents of a young child, would not be human if they did not want him to become a certain type of person and achieve certain goals. The danger is that they may impose their *own* standards on the child, which may not be right for him at all. What he gets out of life and the person he becomes should be the result of his own desires and efforts, directed and abetted by the parents — in diminishing doses as he matures.

The hopes and desires expressed in the statements below represent an attitude based on mutual respect between you and your child, a recognition of the spiritual values in life, a good deal of common sense, and a great deal of love.

We want our child to develop, both mentally and physically, to the fullest extent of his capability.

We want him to recognize and follow his own inclinations — to "do his own thing."

We hope he will learn to appreciate the beauty and fineness that exist around him, and to recognize the evils. In other words, we hope he will learn to discriminate.

We do not want to limit him, or to overstimulate him, by imposing our views on him. We want him to develop his own standards and goals and to work toward them in his own way.

We hope he will become a person who values his spiritual achievements more than his worldly ones.

We hope, of course, that he will learn a trade or profession — of his own choosing — that will provide him with adequate physical comfort. Far more important — one that will provide him with mental and moral satisfaction.

Finally, we hope that he will be honest, courageous, considerate, tolerant, self-confident, loyal, and blessed with a sense of humor.

How can we help our child to develop those qualities, and achieve those goals?

"Of his own choosing" may possibly be the most important phrase in the statements above. Let's take the case of Walter H. His father — a widower — was a psychiatrist. He was handsome, intelligent, and catered to a clientele of wealthy, neurotic women. His fondest dream, he repeated endlessly, was that Walter follow in his footsteps.

He took every opportunity to point out how much "good" he was doing in the world, how he filled such an enormous need, and the sacrifices he made to serve his patients.

As Walter matured, he became more and more disgusted with his father's self-justifications. He became aware of the real "needs" in the world, and although anxious to go into medicine, was determined that he would serve the underprivileged. When he announced to his father that he hoped to become an internist in a city hospital rather than a psychiatrist with a private practice, a series of battles began. In the end, his father refused to finance his medical training.

Walter severed all communication with his father. Determined to stick to his course, he managed to finance his own education through scholarships and by taking years off to work and save. This training took ten years instead of the usual seven or eight. He has finally achieved his goal, but the toll in time, in over-work, and in the alienation from his father can never be retrieved. His father, too, has suffered loneliness and remorse but was too stubborn to "give in."

Stories like this are all too common, and what a waste it is! The effort exerted to push Walter into a field he cared nothing about, could have been so well expended. Had his father not been pigheaded in his demands and tried so hard to mold his son into the image *he* had built up, and had he encouraged Walter to the same extent in the area of his choice, he would never have lost his son as he did. Furthermore, he would have had the satisfaction of helping Walter to become a success as an internist.

In allowing your child to grow, and to develop to the best of his ability, it is terribly important that you do not discourage his efforts — or his good intentions. Your approach to him should be encouraging, sympa-thetic, and constructive. Parents are often unaware that they have withheld encouragement, or discour-aged a commendable impulse.

Last Mother's Day my neighbor's four-year-old boy, Tommy, was playing in his yard and he saw a particu-larly pretty flower in the garden. He was too young to have bought his mother a present, but he had seen his

older sister give her a gift, so he pulled up the flower
— roots and all — and ran to give it to Mom. Instead
of thanking him, she scolded him for ruining the plant.
Her reaction may possibly prevent him from pulling
up more plants by the roots, but it will surely discourage any warm impulse to give her a flower again. Far
better if she had thanked him for his thoughtfulness,
and explained that if he pulled up plants in that way
there would be no more flowers to enjoy in the future.
She might then have taken him to the garden with a
pair of scissors, shown him how to cut the blooms
properly, and let him help her make an arrangement
of them. He would see that, when cut and put in water
at once, flowers last and give pleasure for several days,
while those pulled out whole and allowed to dry up,
quickly droop.

She also missed an opportunity to include another
very valuable lesson — that love is not best expressed
by giving in to a sudden impulse. The expression of love
is of much more value if care and preparation have
gone into its manifestation. This is not a lesson which
one could explain to a four-year-old, but the message
is there for him to recognize. It is very important for
children to learn that, even though their basic impulses are instinctively right, these instincts must be
properly restrained and channeled with planning and

thought. By making a little effort, Tommy's mother might well have turned his misdeed into a profitable lesson, and by showing her appreciation would have encouraged, rather than stifled, his natural generosity.

Applause and appreciation of your child's successes are important, and so is avoidance of dwelling on his failures. Even more important is encouragement while he is on the way. Your opinion must be sincere and not evasive, but it is not dishonest — and it is extremely helpful — to play up the good aspects of his plans and to play down the bad.

Do your very best to encourage your youngster in those skills and hobbies that are to his own particular liking. Too many people exert their influence on a child by discouraging certain enthusiasms because they are not of interest to the people themselves. Even if your child's scheme or project seems impractical or ridiculous, don't tear it down at once. Encourage him to tell you about it, and keep your opinion to yourself until he is finished. Very often, if the plan is truly impossible, this will come through to him as he tries to put it into words. If there *is* some merit in it, you can then help him to pull out the worthwhile aspects, and with your help and enthusiasm his project may become a reality.

Words of thanks, approval, and praise are as impor-

tant to children as they are to adults. Almost all of us
remember our manners with strangers — we rarely
forget our pleases and thank-yous with mere acquaintances. But how often do we openly praise or express
our appreciation to our own families? We are quick to
express our displeasures but very slow to speak out of
our pleasure. We are often overly anxious to discourage and loath to give any encouragement at all. For
special efforts, or a job well done, there is no reward
more satisfying than sincere praise. A child should be
given it unstintingly whenever he merits it; frequently
enough so that he is firmly convinced that his parents
are impressed not only when he succeeds, but when
he *tries* his best to do well.

Part of your job in helping your youngster to grow
into a well-adjusted adult is to teach him the limits of
his own importance. He must, of course, receive the
love and encouragement he needs to develop self-confidence and a recognition of his place — first in the
family, later in the community. He must also learn
that those around him are equally deserving (or more
so) and that they have their places, too.

Ideally, a parent's interest in his child should be
there, available to be called upon, but it should not be
overly possessive or omnipresent. Your appraisal must,

of course, be completely honest of both yourself and your child, but it should not be disparaging.

Most of us have known women who can talk about nothing but their children. They regale their dinner partners with little Tommy's latest bon mot, they call their mothers to report each new word he utters, and they drive their friends to distraction with detailed descriptions of every daily crisis or triumph. These misguided souls are doing themselves a double disservice. They will soon find their friends are avoiding them and invitations are fewer and fewer. And poor little Tommy, through no fault of his own, is becoming the most unpopular child in Midville. If you find yourself falling into this trap, remind yourself of this remark made by a male friend of mine after a miserable dinner hour: "There's no use in talking to anyone about your children. They either have some of their own or they don't."

Any normal youngster will start to show off when he is put in the limelight, and any child who is forever showing off is a bore and a pest. Consistency in this area is most important. It is not fair to a child to pay no attention to his behavior when he is alone with you or the family, and then to put him on a stage when he is among visitors. He will naturally go to any length to win their applause, especially if he has been starved for it at other times. In the same vein, it is not fair that a visitor's disapproval or criticism should lead you to punish your child for something he has always been allowed to do when alone with you.

2

Basic Attitudes

Your Relationship with Your Child

When you and your husband have figured out who your baby is, what you are to him, and what you want for him, you are ready to decide what sort of relationship you wish to develop. It will, necessarily, change as the baby develops, but you should form some sort of goal toward which you plan to work.

Do you, for example, want your relationship to be based on comradeship or companionship, or do you prefer the idea of "togetherness"? These words sound very similar, and yet there are important shades of difference. Togetherness is just what it implies — being together physically, as well as mentally. It implies a similarity in emotional reactions, and in the thinking process. Togetherness is the logical relationship for a mother and a very young baby. She *is* with him constantly, and he is dependent entirely on her actions and thoughts. His emotional reactions are bound to be very similar to hers; fear when she is afraid, joy when she laughs, tears when she is angry.

Comradeship or companionship develop as the child's own personality begins to emerge. By the time he is a year old, he is no longer just a reflection of his mother, but he establishes his own identity. His thoughts and emotions often run quite contrary to hers. Total "togetherness" begins to disintegrate, and that is as it should be. I know that after the first months, I did not always want to be "together" with my children — nor they with me.

Comradeship is very similar to companionship — in fact, the dictionary gives each word as a synonym for the other. But to me, "comrade" has a slightly military air, and "companion" is warmer and closer. It sounds "softer" and would indicate a relationship which would not be too demanding, but would be reliable and satisfying. It is the relationship which I would choose to arrive at ultimately — gradually developing it from the toddler stage to adulthood. At first it will be entirely up to you to establish the degree of companionship, but your child will play a growing role, as he matures, in determining not only the quantity, but the quality, of your relationship.

The Question of Precedence

You must also decide where he is going to fit into your life in order of importance. To what extent will he take precedence? Which, for example, is more important: getting to the bank to cash a check before closing time, or helping Bobby to find his bathing trunks so that he can go swimming in your neighbor's pool? Getting your hair done to cheer yourself up after a frustrating day, or taking Billy to the park because he, too, is bored or unhappy after an uninteresting morning at nursery school?

There are no pat answers to these questions. Sometimes it is more important that *you* get dressed up rather than Billy. Otherwise, you may simply "take it out" on him — making his day even more miserable. Or perhaps the deliverymen will refuse to leave the new refrigerator unless you have the cash that you must get from the bank before two-thirty.

The crux of the matter is not what you decide to do, but your *reason* for that decision. Is it honest? Is it really necessary to get to the bank, or could it wait until tomorrow? Does your hair truly look that dreadful, or are you just using that as an excuse because you can't face going to the park?

These questions are going to come up every day, in one form or another. Sometimes you will decide in your own favor and sometimes in your child's. That is perfectly acceptable, because life will treat him the same way. Some days luck will be with him and some days it won't. But as far as you are concerned, if your decisions are honest (except for those occasional, excusable times when things pile up and you say, "The heck with it — I've had it — I'm damned if I'll go to the park today!), nine times out of ten you will come up with the decision which is right for you *and* your child.

It is a question of perspective, too. Are you going to let your youngster run your life, are you going to run his, or will it be a little of each? Hopefully you will take both of your needs into consideration. The mother who jumps to acquiesce to every one of her child's demands is doing neither him nor herself a favor. Nor, of course, is the parent who says, "I'm bigger, I'm older, and we'll do it *my* way." Fair is fair, and when one of these "conflicts of interests" comes along, weigh both sides of the question. Be sure you are being honest, be sure you are giving your youngster a fair deal, and be sure he won't have any reason to think, when he's old enough, "Oh, that's just another of Mother's excuses!"

Mutual Respect

Common sense tells us that successful training cannot be accomplished without your child's cooperation. To win his confidence, and thereby his willingness to go along with you, you must establish rapport — and mutual respect. This is not done by means of orders — "Do this!" "You can't do that," and so on. That can only lead to resistance and rebellion. It is essential that you create an atmosphere in which you are the leader, and yet still a partner. Rather than "Do it that way," *suggest* "Let's try it this way." For example: For some time Timmy's mother had been trying to make him lower his voice. In her exasperation, she was talking louder and louder herself. One day she caught herself actually yelling, "Timmy, stop shouting!" "Timmy, be *quiet!*" Recognizing her mistake, she whispered, "Timmy, let's play a game — let's see who can talk the quietest." She renewed the contest frequently, and

Timmy's habit was gradually broken, with no resentment on his part. She succeeded by making him a partner in the effort.

The way you speak to your child — the tone of your voice as well as your words — when he is learning to talk is of prime importance. He will, if he is normal, learn to talk more or less fluently in his second and third years. It will be the most demanding intellectual task he may ever face. Language is an indication of the very root of our intelligence — it is the ability to arrange artificial sounds and symbols into a pattern that can be understood — that allows us to think and to communicate. Your child will copy your every word and inflection, and to the best of his ability, the way you express your thoughts. Therefore, your manner of speaking to him affects not only the way he will speak himself, but to a large extent the way he is going to think, and as a result, behave. If you talk to him in an authoritative, declarative manner — "Do this!" "Don't do that!" — you are teaching him that that is the way to get what he wants, or to prevent what he doesn't want.

The richness of life as well as the richness of language depend on the options that are open to us. To constantly demand leaves no option. To say, "Let's try this" or "Why don't we do it this way?" is to offer a choice. It helps to develop a mind that recognizes an option and therefore the need to think and discriminate.

This process is directly related to the etiquette with which this book is concerned. The request instead of the demand offers a way of life through which one can get what one wants in a civilized way, offering options for others (consideration), and thus, indirectly, for oneself. The difference between "Give me my dinner" and "Would you please pass me my plate?" reflects far more than a difference in manners — or polish; it represents a real cultural — and character — difference. The first statement denies the existence of anyone else except as a means to an end. The second remark acknowledges another's existence, and shows a willingness to communicate beyond a mere means of survival. The former is not only harsh and rude — it is essentially selfish and "alone." The latter is more human because it acknowledges or invites communication and implies that the other person has the option of refusal. The first is the statement of a person who feels he is alone against the world. The second is the voice of someone who knows he is a part of the world, and recognizes its needs as well as his own.

While your child is still a baby, he must, of course, learn to obey certain commands without question, and immediately: *"No,* Hank" or *"Come back,* Susie" may save Hank from burning his finger on the hot stove, or keep Susie from running in front of a car. The order would be of little use if you stopped to qualify or explain — the damage would already be done. So your youngster must learn that at times, instant obedience is expected. You will generally convey this urgency involuntarily through the tone of your voice. In an emergency you will speak loudly and sharply, and that is as it should be, because the warning will be communicated to your child.

If he is accustomed to language and tone of voice which acknowledge him as a person, and offer him a choice of response, the occasional use of the imperatives "No" and "Don't" will stand out. He will come to realize that in most cases we can do things in a variety of ways; we can take our time to choose what is best or most pleasant for each person. But he will also learn that there are instances and situations where he has no choice; he simply cannot put his fingers into an electrical outlet or jump into water that is over his head. If, however, you overuse the imperative, constantly shouting "Don't" when "Let's not" would do just as well, your child will soon learn that there are rarely any harsh results from violating or ignoring a "Don't" — and this will have serious consequences.

Courtesy Is a Pleasure and a Privilege

One of the most important things you can do to start your child on the road to thoughtful, gracious behavior is to instill in him the idea that courtesy *is* a privilege and it *can* be a pleasure. You can begin to do this from the time he is a very small child — even though you may think he is too young to notice. Tiny children observe and absorb at a much tenderer age than most people realize. If, for example, Betsy's mother always stops whatever she is doing and goes to the door to kiss her husband good-bye in the morning, it will seem quite natural to Betsy to kiss her mother good-bye when she leaves for nursery school. At night when Dad comes home, Mom always gets up and goes to greet him. It isn't long before Betsy is dropping her toys and running to give him a hug and a kiss, too. If parents greet each other as if each meeting were a real pleasure — something worth a little effort, perhaps — the children — who miss nothing — will want to do the same. Each time they do, family affection is strengthened.

The small courtesies which Father extends to Mother

set an example for their youngsters which is invaluable. If Dad appears to *enjoy* holding the door for Mom or she seems to like to help him on with his heavy coat, the youngsters will consider it a privilege to be allowed to help, too. The challenge is to make those acts seem natural and inevitable, and the secret to that is that they are regarded — or should be regarded — as a pleasure. This is one area in which Father has more opportunity and more responsibility than Mother. In spite of the current attitude that women should, in their new independence, be treated in the same way as men, I believe that youngsters, especially boys, should be brought up to recognize that women — like it or not — are still physically less strong than men. Although women no longer expect to be treated as helpless hothouse flowers, some of the more practical courtesies are desirable and important. When Dad carries a heavy suitcase for Mom, pulls out a chair for her, helps her down slippery steps, he is not denying her independence or self-reliance. He is merely acting in a respectful and protective manner — one which I firmly believe should be fostered in his children. This attitude should be instilled in young boys and girls regarding adults — both men and women. Because youngsters have more strength and endurance than their elders they can and should learn that the performing of these courtesies is not only something that must be done, but is a privilege and a pleasure.

Running errands or complying with other requests can be a privilege, too, if the demand is made in the right way. Mr. D. rarely meets with any opposition when he wants his children to bring him a cool drink or close the window for him. He never says, "Annie, get me a Coke." He says, "Oh, Annie, I'm *so* tired. A drink of Coke would certainly make me feel a lot better." Annie has to run to get to the refrigerator before her younger brother, Teddy, can get there first. Their dad has made them feel needed and important to him, and they vie for the honor of doing him a favor. The courtesy he asks has been presented as a privilege, not a demand, and the idea that doing something *for* someone is a pleasure is firmly imbedded.

A word of warning is in order: Don't overdo it! Your youngster will soon realize he is being tricked. It works as long as you don't try it too often. If you do, he will begin to think "politeness" is simply a way of getting people to do things they don't want to do. Good manners will become just a phony game — a means of getting your own way.

Trust Your Child's Motives

In order to understand your child's motives, it is often essential to use your imagination to the full. A little child's mind does not work in the same channels as an adult's, and you must often go far outside what seems logical or rational at a moment of extreme tension. I recently saw a young mother, whose child had just darted into the street to save his little brother's ball from being run over, grab the child and spank him unmercifully on the spot. The boy's motive was unimpeachable, but in carrying out his thoughtful impulse, he endangered his life, disobeyed strict instructions about running into the street, and scared his mother out of her wits. To be sure, she forgot about his motive because of her terror, and through anger that he should have caused her such terror. But it was a normal human reaction, and one that was not without value in itself. Any rule which involves a matter of actual safety — life and death perhaps — must be enforced without mercy. Billy had been repeatedly told not to run into the street, but until he actually did it and felt the violence of his mother's reaction, it had not seemed especially important to him. After that incident, he will think twice before disobeying that particular rule again. Since, in this case, the importance of the possible consequences far outweighed the importance of his motive, and also since he was actually disobedient, his mother's reaction was not only understandable, but justifiable.

In a similar case a little girl, Jennie, was left alone while her mother ran to the store on a quick errand. Having heard her mother say that she didn't feel well and had chills, Jennie thought she would light the fire and have the room nice and warm for Mommy when she got home. She lighted it, and piled more and more wood on until the roaring flames started a chimney fire. Jennie, in spite of her thoughtfulness, was severely punished. While again in this instance, the motive behind the deed was thoughtfulness, the danger of Jennie's disobedience to previous instructions about not lighting matches made strong measures necessary. Can you, in any case, imagine Jennie's mother, after seeing the smoke pouring from the chimney, come running in and saying, "How sweet of you, Jennie, to have the room all cozy and warm for me!" Of course not! Natural emotions such as fear and anger make your child realize that you are a fellow human being — and he or she is not looking for an unbelievable, untouchable idol.

Once the crisis is over, emotions have cooled, and the sore bottoms have stopped stinging, it is a good idea to sit down with your child and explain the reason for your vehemence. This is not an attempt to justify your actions — you don't need to do that — but to point out the connection between the punishment and the crime, the reasons for the severity.

For every example of the nature of the two above, however, there are a hundred situations where a child's motives should be appreciated more than they are. Hasn't your child ever broken a glass or a plate when she was trying to help you set the table or dry the dishes? If so, did you yell at her, "Oh, Mary, how stupid of you! Put the dishes down — I'll set the table myself"? Or did you say, "Mary, let me show you how you should have held the glass. Then, next time we set the table together, there won't be any accidents"? If your reaction was like the first, you will quickly destroy any desire on Mary's part to help you. She will feel only shame at her awkwardness, and resentment that you should be angry at what was obviously a mistake. If, however, you manage to control your annoyance, you will relieve her embarrassment, and encourage her by intimating that you will enjoy having her help again.

Never forget that your appreciation — your thanks instead of a scolding — will help to convince her that courtesy *is* a pleasure.

Trust Your Child's Integrity

Most children can take accusations from outsiders in their stride — whether the accusations are true or false. But a false accusation from a parent who has jumped to a conclusion inspired by circumstantial evidence — without waiting to hear the child's side of the story — can be a devastating blow. It is equally disastrous for you to accept the truth of someone else's accusation rather than your youngster's denial. You may have reason to doubt his word but until you have positive proof that he is the offender, you must give him the benefit of the doubt. If you don't, you will never be able to convince him that trust and loyalty exist between you. The giving of implicit trust can be most difficult at times for parents. A window was broken in Mrs. Harlow's basement last year. Billy Brooks, who lived next door, had been seen enjoying a little "batting practice" in his yard that morning. Mrs. Harlow called

Billy's mother and accused him of the act. Billy denied it emphatically, and his mother and father took his word that he was innocent. They told Mrs. Harlow politely but firmly that they believed Billy, and would take no responsibility for the damage. Relations between the neighbors were admittedly strained for several weeks until a delivery man who had not been in the area for some time heard about the window and reported that he had seen the accident take place. Although Billy had been there, the true culprit was a much larger boy who lived in the next block. The boy's parents were notified. He confessed, and his parents' insurance covered the accident. They reimbursed Mrs. Harlow, who apologized to the Brookses. Had Billy's mother and father mistrusted him and accepted Mrs. Harlow's word against his, he would have justifiably felt insulted, hurt, and rejected. As it is, Mrs. Harlow and other neighbors, as well as Billy's parents, are aware that he is on the way to becoming a reliable, trustworthy adult. And Billy himself is secure, knowing that he has that invaluable gift — his parents' trust.

Credit Where Credit Is Due

Most parents do not give enough credit where credit is due. They assume, because Billy is showing no evidence of absorbing what they have been teaching him about table manners, that he has learned nothing. This is not necessarily so. Their nagging approach or their derogatory attitude may simply have gotten Billy's "back up" so that he doesn't *wish* to comply. And yet when he goes over to his friend Ward's house for supper, Ward's mother calls the next day to tell Billy's mother what lovely manners he has! Don't be discouraged if *your* Billy doesn't seem to be progressing. Try to *encourage* him by making your attitude more positive — with more patience, more praise, and less criticism.

If you let Billy know that you take it for granted that he will have good manners, he undoubtedly *will*. Conversely, if he thinks that you suspect him of not wanting to behave well, he will react by behaving abominably. A constant stream of "Do this, don't do that, stand up, say 'thank you,' come here," and so on and so on will soon cause a child to close his ears completely. Billy, who may have had every intention of saying "thank you" without being reminded, becomes annoyed and resentful at the implication that he doesn't know how to behave. Some instruction, and repetition of it, is necessary of course, but you must continually imply that you assume he will live up to your expectations.

He is going to make mistakes, and you might as well face up to that. Accept the fact that slipups and forgetfulness are necessary, because without them, you would have little direction for your instruction, and your child would have nothing to learn.

The Most Important "Don'ts"

Many of the most important attributes of a good parent are negative rather than positive. A mother or father must recognize the restraints and restrictions that are necessary as well as the positive actions.

There isn't a mother in the world who hasn't wanted to show off her baby's accomplishments or charms to friends and relatives. Giving in to this urge occasionally is a good thing. It is good for the child's self-confidence and self-respect and it is good for the parents' ego. However, to do so continually has the opposite effect. The child becomes a stuck-up little "brat," and the mother becomes a crashing bore. The first "don't," therefore, is don't make a habit of attracting attention to your child.

The second is similar: Don't talk about your child in front of him. "I do wish I could keep Debbie out of the cookie jar. She is getting so fat it's repulsive." "Your Jeannie's hair is so curly and pretty. I can't do a thing with Nancy's — it's so lanky and straight." No grown person in his right mind would make this sort of re-mark about another adult in the subject's hearing, and yet I have heard mothers do it time and again in front of their children. Do they forget that youngsters have ears too, and feelings that can be hurt? You have every right, and often good reason, to discuss your child's shortcomings with friends who may offer helpful ad-vice or sympathy, but do it when your youngster is not around. He cannot possibly believe you have much respect or admiration for him if he overhears remarks which are insulting both in content and in the fact that their very utterance indicates he is too stupid to under-stand.

Don't break your word — whether it is a promise of

something pleasant, or a threat of punishment. The latter, especially, can result in a total lack of discipline. Children are very smart — far more so than they are often given credit for — and they soon learn to recognize a threat which is not plausible, or a promise which will never be carried out.

"Teddy, if you do that once more, you're not going to play with Bobby again this summer!" Or, "If you don't finish your cereal right now, no more television this week!" These threats are totally unrealistic and Teddy knows it. Bobby lives next door, and it would be next to impossible to keep the boys separated all summer. And television is far too valuable a "sitter" for Teddy's mother to carry out the second threat. Had she said "for the rest of the day" or "for a week" instead of "this summer" Teddy would have known that she meant it, and her word and her authority would be unquestionable. So, just as you must think twice about making a pleasant promise that you are not sure you can keep, you must be even more careful about promising to inflict an unenforceable penalty.

If you are not absolutely sure you can keep a promise, *don't make it.* A promise is almost always something to look forward to; and a broken promise usually involves a disappointment — something that your child has anticipated or counted on which will not happen.

There are times when circumstances combine to make it impossible to keep a promise, and you will help to alleviate the shock and dismay if you can make your youngster understand the reason. He may seem to reject your explanation at the time, but if you do your level best to make him "see," and also, if possible, to offer an easier-to-fulfill alternative, you will be able to preserve his faith in you.

Deliberate deception is slightly different from breaking your word but it is an even more dangerous weapon for destroying confidence. Never tell a child that you will be downstairs in the kitchen while he takes his nap, when you have every intention of going out to visit with your neighbor. You might not be "caught," but should he wake up with a tummy-ache and call for you or go looking for you, his faith in your word would suffer an irreparable blow. If you are called to go out for an unavoidable reason — perhaps to pick up a sick child from school — it is better to wake the sleeper up and bundle him into the car than to take the chance of his waking up in an empty house after you had told him you would be there.

Don't betray your child's confidence. If you are honest and dependable in all your dealings with your child, his confidence will never be misplaced. There is another meaning, however, which should be mentioned.

That is, never betray to another anything your child says in confidence to you. Have you ever, as I have, heard a mother say, in her child's hearing, "Betsy said the cutest thing yesterday. . . ." Poor Betsy, who didn't think of her remark as "cute," and may well have meant it only for her mother's ears, is indignant and embarrassed. If it happens frequently, she will soon learn to keep her thoughts to herself, and spontaneous communication between her and her mother will gradually be lost.

A child's secrets are, or should be, as inviolable as those of an adult. If your little girl or boy has enough trust in you to confide his innermost thoughts and opinions, or share with you something which he does not believe would reach other ears, you must never betray that trust. If you feel the information he has is reliable and the situation requires someone else's participation, never, never, go behind his back to reveal his secret. Explain to him *why* it is essential for someone else to know, and if possible, persuade him to tell whoever is concerned. In that way he can count on you not to betray his confidence, and he can also count on your support when it is necessary.

The last "don't" on my list is rather different. It does not affect discipline or behavior, but it can have a lasting effect on character. Don't talk "down" to your child

— and most of all, *don't* talk "baby talk." Never underestimate his intelligence. Let him know that you don't by talking to him as an equal. Naturally, you must use simple words and simple phrases to a baby, but they should be spoken in the language you use to everyone else. Baby talk can be habit-forming, too, and can be terribly embarrassing to the child as he gets older and recognizes it — and its implications. The same is true of giving a baby a nickname which, if it sticks, may be a detriment to him all his life. An adult man or woman who is still known as "Bobsy" or "Baby-Doll" because a doting mother thought it sounded cute, has been saddled with a real burden, and one that is often very hard to shed.

Life Is Not Always Fair

In teaching children to be fair themselves, it is also necessary to teach them that *life is not always fair*. It is a hard lesson, but one that confronts every child sooner or later. If he has occasionally been subjected to unfairness at home, where presumably there was some good reason for it, at least it will be a little easier to accept later on, at school, among friends, and so on.

No matter how hard you may try, it is almost impossible to feel exactly the same about all your children. Most parents will not admit it — even to themselves — but they like one child better than another. Although it is not always true, a mother often tends to favor the child who is more obedient, more cooperative, or perhaps, simply more handsome. She may not *love* him more, but she will be more ready to grant his requests, and slower to punish him. His brothers or sisters, quite naturally, call this unfair.

Perhaps it is unfair at the time, but the end result will benefit the other children more than the one who is favored. He may be happiest during the years his mother dotes on and protects him, but he will have a harder lesson to learn when he finds that the rest of the world does not necessarily share her admiration. His brothers and sisters, who have had to fight harder for their share of attention, and have learned to accept some unfair knocks in the process, are actually better prepared for life. So don't worry about it too much if you cannot always be one hundred percent fair.

The mother who makes a fetish of being exactly fair *all* the time is, in truth, doing her children a disservice. Mrs. Williams cooked a batch of fudge and divided it into squares. When Tommy and Joe came home from school, she gave them each a piece. Tommy immediately started to whine: "Joe's piece is bigger — why can't I have one like his?" His mother, rather than saying, "There's not *that* much difference," or, "Next time maybe you'll get the bigger one," carefully cut a quarter of an inch slice off the next piece and gave it to Tommy — to make it *exactly* fair. Both boys would have received a better lesson about the realities of life if she had let it go as it was.

There is another area in which you cannot make things fair, but you can help your child to accept the unfairness. That is in the case of his natural attributes or abilities. You cannot change the fact that Debbie is gangly and five feet tall when she is twelve, nor can you make Jamie, who is totally uncoordinated, into a star basketball player. You *can*, with love and understanding, give them confidence and build up their ego. You can help Debbie develop her own interests and skills in art to the extent that she will no longer worry about temporarily being taller than the boys in her class, and you or your husband can encourage Jamie to play the guitar so well that he has an accomplishment of which he can be justly proud. When they have setbacks and Debbie says, "Oh, all I want is to have a boy ask me for a date," or Jamie moans, "I just want to go with the team to play against Foothills," you must be on hand to point out that while it may not seem fair that those things are not for them just now, that's life. These are facts they just have to accept, and learning to take them in stride will help youngsters to become tolerant, courageous adults.

Fairness and Sportsmanship

We *do,* of course, want our children to "play fair" — with us, with their contemporaries, and with themselves. As in all other areas of child-rearing, the parents' example is of prime importance. It is not "fair," for example, to expect a youngster to uphold standards which you do not honor yourself. And you must, of course, practice what you preach. If you want your child to grow up judging his friends and acquaintances fairly — completely impartially — you must do the same within your family.

Sportsmanship is akin to playing fair, and every youngster should be taught the basic precepts. There is no more derogatory accusation or nothing more damaging to a child's popularity than being known as a poor sport. The parents who do not teach their child to be a fair competitor and a good loser are not being fair to him. The code of sportsmanship has three aspects, all of which can be taught by example, by correction, and by patient instruction. It is every parent's duty to instill the following lessons in his child's mind.

Winning

A winner shows his pleasure, of course, but briefly. He takes his win in stride, and does not give it too much importance. He *never* derides or laughs at his opponent. In a team game he gives his teammates or partner full credit and shares all acclaim with them.

Losing

The loser has a harder fight. He must accept his loss gracefully — giving the winner his due and offering congratulations. He must blame only himself for his loss — neither his luck nor his partner's errors. He must never sulk, let his temper get out of hand, or make excuses.

Enjoying sports — win or lose

The youngster who is a welcome member of any team or is always in demand to take part in a game is the one who plays because he enjoys it. He wants to win, of course (or he would be no good as a competitor) but the fun of playing is even more important. He keeps his temper under control — he retains his sense of humor, and he is always ready for a return match.

Another weakness that you, as parents, must guard against is biased or unfair judgment. Don't let your love for your child influence you, or you will destroy his faith in your good sense as well as your fairness. If you allow yourself to be convinced that Susie's teacher was mean or unfair to her, when you know perfectly well that Susie got exactly what she deserved, your advice to her will automatically be wrong.

You must, of course, give Susie a chance to state her case. "Tell me exactly what happened, Susie. What makes you think Miss Goldfarb was unfair?" When you have heard all she has to say — and you must listen carefully — it is up to you to render the fairest judgment you possibly can. If you agree that Miss

Goldfarb was unfair, tell Susie so, and also tell her what she can do to avoid similar incidents in the future. If you feel Susie was at fault, you must tell her that, too, and why you think she was wrong. Only by rendering judgment with complete impartiality can you teach your child to do the same. If the matter is serious enough, you and your husband should go and talk to Miss Goldfarb, but in every case be sure that the verdict is given careful consideration, and is, to the best of your ability, one hundred percent fair.

3

The Earliest Lessons

Every successful parent recognizes — early in the game — the importance of good, honest discipline. Discipline is the first lesson your child must accept and learn — from the moment he begins to understand you at all. I don't mean discipline in the sense of punishment, but rather self-discipline, which is the foundation of a strong, dependable character. This is not as harsh as it may sound, because discipline can be accepted with very little conscious effort on the part of your youngster — if his training begins in the earliest weeks of his life.

The first step toward discipline is obedience. There are two types of obedience — one of tremendous value in developing strength of character, and the other extremely harmful to a child's personality. The first is *willing* obedience. If a child feels confidence in, and security with, the person who is making the demand — the parents, in the case of a very young child — obedience will be given without resentment. He will even come to understand, in due course, that obedience is beneficial to him.

The other type is obedience *through fear*. You have surely seen a puppy that has been beaten into submission, cowering and cringing at the sound of its master's voice. The effect on a child's personality is the same, and obedience which is enforced too harshly will soon destroy any desire on the part of the child to cooperate.

If your child, in his earliest months, becomes accustomed to adapting himself to the family's schedule and to the demands made on him, he will progress naturally from conforming with your pattern of obedience to you, then to his teachers, and finally to all those in authority who earn his respect. During this progression you must not expect "blind" obedience. If you have kept communication and exchange of knowledge and opinion open from the beginning he will be learning to discriminate, and to decide for himself who, and what, is worthy of his obedience.

You may ask, "What do obedience, schedules, thumb-sucking, toilet-training — all subjects discussed in this chapter about early training — have to do with etiquette? They are physical habits or needs, and how can they be related to manners?"

The answer goes back to the true concept of etiquette — consideration. The considerate person fits in — he is a welcome *part* of society, never an outsider. To do this he must learn to comply with the wishes of the majority — in the case of a young child, his family. In this light, the value of the schedule is obvious. Rather than being a disruptive influence, he enhances the pleasure of the family when he has learned to adjust to its habits, and this is very much in line with the aims of etiquette.

Toilet-training is somewhat different in that it will not change the family schedule if it is not enforced. But the child who runs around with dirty, smelly diapers is hardly attractive, and making oneself attractive is definitely a part of good manners. It is also a matter of consideration for the youngster's mother. He should be made to understand that when he learns to use the toilet, he will be helping to make life easier for her. Bed-wetting follows the same pattern. It is not an action which will contribute to the happiness of the family, as it makes life more difficult for those responsible for the child's care. The connection, therefore, is not in the actual habits discussed, but in the effect they will have on others, as well as on the child himself. That is what etiquette is primarily concerned with — the interrelationships of people. Good manners, whether eating when you are expected to (keeping a schedule) or simply saying "please" or "thank you," are merely a means of improving those relationships.

The Value of a Schedule

The more a baby's schedule can be adhered to in the first weeks of his life, the better chance he has to develop tranquillity and stability. For many years babies were invariably fed at six, ten, two, six, and ten, and put to bed immediately after each feeding. This worked beautifully in many cases, but in others, parents wondered why their child was perpetually fretful and restless. For at least twenty years, pediatricians and parents have realized that some babies require more frequent feeding, others sleep more soundly if kept up for some time after a meal, and so on. Now it is not necessarily considered a sign of temper or impatience when a child starts crying for his bottle an hour before it is due. To "give in" and feed the baby early had long been considered "spoiling him." Today we know that children's needs vary, and a baby who cries regularly before his meal probably needs food sooner than one who contentedly waits four or five hours.

This does not mean that schedules should be abandoned. Far from it! It merely means that a schedule should be established which will keep the baby happy and comfortable — one adjusted to his particular needs. However, it must also be planned so that his care does not upset the lives of the rest of the family. If, in the beginning, it seems that the hours the baby needs food interfere with family meals, his feeding hours must be gradually but steadily moved back or ahead so that his mother can devote her entire time and attention to him when he most needs it. Because it seemed necessary to feed him at 7:00 P.M. when he first came home from the hospital, does not mean that he must be fed at 7:00 P.M. indefinitely. Each day his mealtime can be advanced (or delayed) by an almost imperceptible five or ten minutes, until his regular hour is eight o'clock, for example, when dinner is over and his mother can relax and enjoy him. Nothing could be worse for the baby — or for his brothers and sisters — than to make the entire household schedule revolve around him.

After the first few weeks, the baby's schedule will become subject to more and more interruptions. His mother will often have to take him with her when she goes out, other children in the family will become less concerned about making noise and waking him, and his parents will be less cautious about disturbing him to "show him off" to visitors. But every effort should be made to make these interruptions occur during his "play" hours, rather than nap — or meal — time. All these experiences are good for the child. The sooner he is exposed to changing conditions and a variety of faces, the more easily he will adapt to new situations. To retain a schedule is one thing — it is another, and very wrong, to isolate him.

A mother who feeds her child snacks at any hour to keep him quiet or picks him up out of his playpen every time he starts to fuss, is asking for trouble. If she cannot resist his cries for long enough to let him know that his every demand cannot and will not be instantly met, she will soon find herself doing nothing but "waiting on" her child. He must learn that certain things happen at certain times, and his deliberate bad behavior is not going to change it.

Events occur in every household which make interruption of schedules or relaxation of discipline inevitable. When a child is ill, no mother in her right mind would expect him to eat or sleep in his normal pattern. Nor, when mother and father go away, and a doting grandmother is left in charge, would we expect normal discipline to be maintained. If the illness is protracted, or grandmother's visit prolonged, it may be some time before a return to a normal schedule is achieved. But it must be done, if peace and orderliness are to be maintained, even though it requires a period of "sitting it out" while the baby tests you by asserting himself as he did during the emergency.

You may well be people who do not like living on a schedule yourselves, and that is certainly your prerogative. But although you enjoy irregular hours, and haphazard living, don't expect your baby to do the same. Very small children usually *like* living according to schedule, and they do not feel it restrictive to be fed, bathed, and put to bed at more or less the same time each day. Instead, it gives them a feeling of security and peace to live in an orderly atmosphere. Later, they may adopt your pattern by choice — especially as their interests become more widespread, and their activities more varied. But for the sake of your baby's peace of mind, and to keep confusion and tension away from him until he has a stable start, you can do him no greater favor than sticking — within reason — to a schedule suited to his temperament and physical needs.

Toilet-training

The most common failing among young parents in regard to toilet-training is showing too much concern. Different children react to this lesson in various ways — some are ready for it far earlier than others. Don't let yourself become upset if your youngster is still wetting himself when he is two and a half, while your neighbor's child, who is eighteen months old, seems to be completely trained.

Your best approach to toilet-training is constant encouragement, and very little discipline. You must, of course, give him ample opportunities to use the toilet. When he is too little to let you know his needs, take him to the bathroom at regular intervals — after meals, before and after naps, and once or twice between. As soon as he can talk, try to get him to let you know when he wants to go by asking him at regular intervals. When he makes mistakes, as he will for many weeks or months, don't make an issue of it, and certainly never punish him. Let him know that you are mildly disappointed, and take him to the bathroom at that time the next day. Praise him each time you find him dry and when he uses the toilet, but don't make *too* much of it. He should know that this is not an unusual achievement, but simply what is desirable and expected of him.

Sometimes a child appears to be totally trained, and suddenly starts wetting his pants again. This is usually caused by a disturbance of some sort in his life — the arrival of a new baby, a move to a new home, or the loss of a parent. Any situation which seems to him to be an upheaval, or to deprive him of his security, may cause this relapse. It may be an emotional reaction which he cannot control, or it may be a demand for more attention. The additional care his mother must give him in changing his pants, or the excitement of the scene he creates, helps him to feel important.

The best possible cure for a relapse is to recognize the reason for it and, insofar as possible, to correct whatever it may be. If the situation is irreversible, as it probably is, you must counteract the child's tension or unhappiness by extra care and attention. Making him feel relaxed and secure is even more vital than it was in the original training period. Only when he does relax, will he go back to the normal process and take up where he left off.

Most children would eventually train themselves if

left alone, partly because it is more comfortable to be clean and dry, and partly because of the reaction of their peers as they get older. Also, as their control develops, they can regulate their needs more efficiently and can use the toilet less often and at more convenient times. All that you are doing, really, is to speed up the process, thereby making the child more comfortable and saving work for yourself. So, while your child is still a toddler, until he is three, perhaps, keep cool about toilet-training. Quiet encouragement and praise will do more than any punishment could possibly achieve.

If your child has refused to be trained by three or four, for whatever reason, you will have to take more drastic steps. While he is very small, you can keep him in disposable diapers with plastic outside, or in diapers and rubber pants. In either case, he can do no damage wherever he may be when he wets himself. But when he is too big for diapers, and you put him into training pants, it may be necessary to lay down some restrictions. As in most other situations, leave him a choice. Since you should not be expected to have your rugs or your chairs stained by his mistakes, you have every right to keep him away from the part of the house which can be damaged. Tell him that it is entirely up to him. He can wet his pants as long as he wants to, but he can *not* do so wherever he wishes. He has a choice of controlling himself, or staying in his own room or outside. You may also tell him that he is going to have to change himself and that you have other things to do. But keep the door open — be sure he knows you are always ready to give help with using the toilet if he needs it, because in that case he is meeting your stipulations.

Your youngster will undoubtedly continue to wet his bed at night long after he has ceased making mistakes during the day. The bladders of very small children are simply not able to make it for such a long stretch. So, for a time, you will simply put your child into training pants during the day, and back into rubber pants or waterproofed diapers at night. To help him get through the night, you can cut down on his liquid intake from suppertime on, and you can pick him up and put him on the toilet just before you go to bed. In due course, if all goes normally, he will start to wake up dry in the morning.

However, many seemingly well-adjusted, healthy youngsters go on wetting their beds at night, even until they are six or seven years old. Undisciplined children may do so because they have been permitted to do anything they want, when they want to. They have not been taught the need for control in any situation, so they do not feel control is necessary in bed.

Mothers and fathers, not unnaturally, may get quite upset when their older child continues to wet his bed. Some youngsters do it because they enjoy the extra fuss and attention. Their parents spend extra time taking them to the bathroom at night, and many hours cajoling, arguing, and discussing their problem.

Other children simply find it more difficult than is normal to control their bladders. If this is the case with your child, it is especially important that you do not criticize or discipline him. He needs encouragement, not punishment. He already feels inferior in that he cannot do what is expected of him, and perhaps what his friends and brothers or sisters do. To add your displeasure and scorn to that unhappiness will only make him more discouraged, and he may give up trying entirely.

The best solution — and it may take a long time to succeed — is to put the problem into his own hands. Convince him that you *know* he is perfectly capable of stopping his habit. Give up all lengthy discussions about the "evils" of bed-wetting, and stop making extra trips to the bathroom during the night, changing his bedding as soon as he wets it, and so on. Take as many measures as necessary, such as rubber sheets to protect the bed or a light left on in the bathroom, to minimize the problem, both for him and for you. Devote yourself to appearing to be unconcerned. Tell him that he may get up and go to the bathroom *without* you, any time he wishes, and he may change his pajamas or his sheets if he is uncomfortable. In short, it is now his problem, not yours. *You* know he can solve it, and you will be happy to help him, and proud of him when he succeeds.

Thumb-sucking

Thumb-sucking falls into the same category as bed-wetting. It is a symptom rather than an illness. It gives a child a pleasant sensation and it also satisfies the sucking urge in a baby. Some children have this urge much more strongly than others. If they continue it too long, it indicates some insecurity or other lack. The limited time that babies are sucking on their bottle, or even on their mother's breast, does not always satisfy them. A pacifier frequently helps, but there is always the danger that the baby will become so dependent on it that he will not be able to give it up. A three- or four-year-old child with a pacifier dangling from its mouth is not particularly attractive, and can even appear retarded. The same danger exists with babies who are constant thumb-suckers.

Desperate parents have tried all sorts of remedies. Occasionally they work — more often they don't. Bitter-tasting, harmless liquids are sold, to be applied to the child's thumb. Some mothers have tried mittens on their child's hand. And a great many more have scolded, pleaded, threatened, and punished. All of these parents are making too much of the problem. Thumb-sucking children do it because they are satisfying a *need*, whether it is for a feeling of security, for more attention, or, perhaps, to compete with a new baby. If you remove their means of satisfying that need abruptly, they will find a substitute, and possibly a far more disastrous one.

If a child does not naturally stop sucking his thumb as he outgrows his bottle and his sucking urge, he will need help to overcome the habit. Once again, don't place too much importance on it. No matter what you have heard, the chances are very slim that he will ruin the shape of his mouth, or develop crooked teeth from it. He *might* if he should continue until he is in grade school, but the chances are equally slim that he will do that. By the time he is in kindergarten the teasing of his own classmates will discourage the habit. Until then, the wisest course is to remind him to stop it, patiently, without criticism, but constantly. It is a *habit* and it is an unconscious one. It is impossible to stop doing something you don't know you are doing, so it is only fair to help him by calling attention to it. The odds are a hundred to one that your child will make up his own mind to stop sucking his thumb suddenly — and he will do it. Don't worry about it until he is starting school, but if he continues after that, ask your pediatrician's advice. He can see the problem in a less emotional way, and he will have had years of experience in helping mothers to help their children break the thumb-sucking habit.

The Validity of "No"

In thinking about how often and in what ways you, as parents, intend to use and enforce nos, you must go back to the question of what is most important to you, and to your child. Looking at the question in that light will give you a useful guideline to follow.

Obviously, for example, the most important no is the

one which will prevent your child from getting hurt or will prevent him from hurting someone else. This is the no which requires instant, unquestioning obedience. It is an infrequent no — reserved for emergencies.

Next in importance, perhaps, is the prohibition against destroying property. With very small children, this no is used very frequently, but if you simultaneously teach them respect for possessions — their own and everyone else's — its use should become unnecessary as they grow older. It is, however, a most important "no" and must be seriously observed in the early years.

From there you go to the more questionable nos — the ones regarding denials or refusals, and here the question of "What's important?" is much more difficult. You must wrestle with your own conscience to decide whether the no you have given was for your own selfish reasons, or for the good of your child. You could not possibly foresee all the circumstances in which you will have to choose between yes and no, but if you ask yourself, honestly, *"Why* am I saying no?" and you answer it with a balanced judgment, you will generally come up with the right answer.

The first specific lesson a baby must learn — for his own safety and for the pleasure of his family — is the

fact that no is inviolable, and cannot, by temper tantrums or other means, be changed to yes.

There are two exceptions to this rule. One is that
a no may be changed to a yes if the reason for the
original denial is removed. When you must refuse a
request, try to foresee the possibility of a change.
Even a tiny child will accept the refusal more readily
if you hold out some hope of a reversal and give him
something to look forward to.

Two-year-old Dickie wanted to play in his sandbox.
"No, Dickie," said his mother. "You have a runny nose
and the sandbox is full of puddles from the rain last
night. I don't want you to get wet, but when the water
dries up, you can go out." Later in the morning the
sun came out, the sand dried up and so did Dickie's
nose, and out he went. His mother's promise of changing no to yes helped to make the time go faster —
even for a toddler of Dickie's age.

This is, of course, a very simplified example, and
many situations arise in which circumstances do
change, but the change could not possibly be foreseen.
In those cases you may not be able to hold out hope
to your child, but you *can* be ready to change your
denial as soon as it becomes possible.

The other acceptable reason for changing a refusal
to a permission is when the person who says no recog-

nizes that he is wrong, and wishes to change his decision. A parent should always be ready to recognize his mistakes, *and admit them.* This is especially important as your child becomes old enough to question the legitimacy of your decisions. Mrs. B., Louise's mother, said Louise could not go downtown with Laurie because she assumed that the little girls were planning to walk by themselves. Sometime later she ran into Laurie's mother, who casually mentioned that she was about to walk downtown with Laurie. Mrs. B. immediately went to find Louise to tell her she might go after all, and why.

In short, when the reason is good and sufficient a no may occasionally be changed to yes. But begging, teasing, sulks, and tantrums are *not* sufficient reason, and a weak inability on a mother's part to stick to her guns can only result in confusion, distrust, and a total lack of discipline.

There are many different kinds of nos, and they vary greatly in importance. There are many meanings, too. No can mean "I can't" or "I don't want to" or "I won't." This is, of course, when no is a response to a demand. It can also be a demand or order in itself, and in that case means, "You can't."

In short, no is used for many different reasons, and to be sure that your no is a legitimate one, you must recognize your own motives for using it. Is it for your child's safety or health? Perfectly legitimate. Is it for the protection of your — or someone else's — property? Also legitimate. Is it to educate the youngster — to help him to learn what is right or wrong or good or bad? This, too, is a "proper" reason for no. *Or,* is it a no of convenience? Are you saying no because it will, for the moment at least, make life easier for you?

It is very easy to fall into the habit of saying no to any request which will cause you inconvenience. When Billy asks, "Can I come to the station with you to meet Daddy?" and you think of the nuisance of getting him into his snowsuit for a ten-minute drive, there is certainly a strong temptation to say, "No, Billy, you stay home and watch TV with Sally." But is this fair to Billy? Wouldn't the pleasure he would get out of keeping you company, and watching the train come in and seeing Dad's smile when he gets to the car, be worth a little extra effort? We are all inclined to take the easy way out, and sometimes out of sheer exhaustion or for other reasons it is permissible, but don't let your laziness shortchange your youngster. Don't let that no of convenience become a habit.

Another *il*legitimate no is the one you may be tempted to use in public. It is difficult for a child who has always been allowed to eat his chicken with his fingers at home to suddenly be told, when you take him to a restaurant, "No, you can't do that." There are, of course, many things which *are* allowable at home which would be foolish or objectionable in public places, but it is your job to prepare your youngster in advance. When he wants to run barefoot in the yard in the summer, tell him when you give him permission, that it's all right here and now in your own neighborhood, but not downtown or at Grandmother's. Explain that there are practical reasons for *not* going barefoot under certain circumstances. Downtown, he might well cut his feet on broken glass or other trash, to say nothing of the filth he could pick up. In Grandma's day, bare feet were considered unsanitary and unspeakable and, simply because you all love and respect her, you would not want to offend her by visiting her shoeless. In other words, insofar as you can foresee it, prepare him for the difference between "in private" and "in public" and don't spring the "social no" on him without warning.

This holds true in your own home, too. If Betsy is allowed to watch television in the living room any time she wishes, what will her reaction be when you tell her no, she must turn it off and go play upstairs when your neighbor drops in to chat? Her reaction will undoubtedly be one of anger at you, and dislike of your neighbor. That is, if you have not prepared Betsy in advance. If she has been told from time to time that she may not watch TV in the living room when guests are there, she will not be taken by surprise. I have been in homes where the children *have* been allowed to continue watching TV, or play loudly and argumentatively in the room where guests were being entertained. A legitimate no would have been in order, not only for the pleasure of the guests, but to teach the children consideration and the fact that they are a part of society — with an obligation to the other members.

By the same token, it is not good training to allow a child privileges in a guest's presence that he does not have at other times. If you allow Peter to stay up an hour later because his aunt and uncle are there, or to do parlor tricks or otherwise show off when you have dinner guests, he will soon take advantage of you every time you entertain. This is another occasion when a firm no will benefit both guests and youngster.

If you wish your influence over your child to continue beyond his early years, you must find a way of keeping it important to him; of not allowing your demands or directions to become stale. There is one vital way to do this — *Don't waste your authority*. If you follow the principle suggested, of putting the stress on the important nos, and avoiding them whenever it seems reasonable, your child will recognize, without argument, when it is a serious no, or when it is a debatable question. Save your ammunition for the important things. Don't resort to the habitual no. The danger of using no too often is the same as that of any other too-frequent repetition. It becomes difficult for you to enforce it in each and every instance, and it becomes boring and meaningless to the child if you do not. Don't ever say no because you don't want to think about a more comprehensive or intelligent answer, or because yes would involve trouble or responsibility you don't want to face.

You must, of course, refuse permission or indicate disapproval many times, but often a softer "I'd rather you didn't" or "I don't think much of that" is sufficient. Firm nos should be reserved for the *important* things. If an answer to a request can be "Maybe later," or "Yes, I'll get you dressed so you can go with me to pick up Daddy," you will be giving hope and pleasure to your child, and saving another no for an occasion which merits it. The fact that you have not used unreasonable nos often will give much more weight to your emphatic no when it is necessary. Even then, your child may not accept it happily, but at least you will avoid that much-too-often-heard groan, "Oh Mother, not again!"

The most important thing to learn about no — for *both* parent and child, is that you mean it. If you do say no when Jimmy says, "Take me with you," stick to it. Whether he kicks and screams, refuses to eat his dinner, or resorts to any other trick he can think of, don't give in. Even though you have conscientiously followed the principle of explaining your no to your child, he will undoubtedly try to "test" you from time to time to be sure you still mean what you say. But if you stand firm, and don't let him get away with it, he will soon accept your no, because he knows, deep down, you have a good reason for it. It's difficult, because it is often far simpler to say, "Well, just this once," than it is to ignore the tantrums or the sullenness. But each time you do it you have punched another hole in the dike of his respect for your word and your dependability.

The Ubiquitous "Why?"

When your youngster is between two and three years old, he will start using conversation as a means of expressing thoughts, rather than simply words to denote a specific object or action. At the same time, he will begin to wonder about things he does not understand, and he will learn how to ask questions. The first and most-often-asked question will be "Why?"

In the very beginning it is not necessary to give a child a reason for requesting obedience. He is too young to listen and understand, and his why is more often than not merely a habit. Your experience, and his lack of it, is sufficient reason for you to make certain requirements.

However, as soon as he is old enough to really think about "Why do I have to?" or "Why can't I?" it is your duty and obligation to give him an understandable reason. At first your answers will be simple — "Because it is dangerous." "Because you'll hurt Molly's feelings if you say that," and so on. As he develops, you will have to explain in more detail, and impress on him the fact that it is not he alone who must obey certain rules. Mom and Dad abide by rules when they play tennis; his big sister keeps the rules at school, and so on. He must learn that you and his sister (and other adults) do not obey laws because of fear of punishment, but because you realize that things work out best for you, and for those around you, if you do. Regulations are necessary if life is to run smoothly and in an orderly fashion, and the adult who automatically stops at a red light or obeys the "Don't Walk" sign, has learned this. When your youngster understands that there are rules for all people of all ages and in all situations, and that the vast majority obeys them without even thinking about it — his obedience, too, will seem natural and inevitable to him.

Some parents ignore the importance of discussion, and their answer to "Why?" is invariably "Because I say so," or "Because I had to do it when I was your age." One is equally as disastrous as the other, and both are a denial that your child is a person. The mother or father who leads a youngster to believe that obedience is simply the imposition of the will of the stronger or bigger on that of the weaker or smaller is creating a dangerous situation. His child, like so many of the "lost" teen-agers today, will either develop a defeatist attitude and attempt to escape from life or will develop a violent and active rebellion against all authority.

4

Courtesy
Starts at Home

The Meaning of Home

What is Home to a child? It is a *place*, but that is not enough. It is *people*, but it must be very special people. Most important, there are *qualities* which turn a house or an apartment into a Home. Love is the basic quality — without it there can be no warmth, and warmth is essential to the atmosphere of Home. Then there are understanding, and trust, and loyalty. And beyond and above all these is the element which makes a family out of individuals and a home out of a house — companionship.

One of the most important things that a home can provide is an *outlet*. It is a place where a child can confide his feelings, go for encouragement, or register his complaints. He can blast off about how he hates his math teacher, or how unfair it is that Jim made the soccer team and he didn't. He can crow a little about making the honor roll, knowing his family will be proud too, whereas his friends would only call it boasting. At home, he knows that his parents and his brothers and sisters are delighted with his achievements, sympathize with his failures, and *care*, one way or another, about his activities. They may disagree with him about many things, but if their house is really a HOME, he knows he will never be doubted or mistrusted, and he will always be listened to and loved. Only at home can he really "let go."

An ideal Home is also a haven or a refuge. It should be a place that a child can come to and know that he will find safety and security, no matter how things may have gone against him at school or at play. He should be able to lower his defenses when he is within his own four walls and drop any shell that he has built to protect himself in public. He may relax, and *be himself*, as he can rarely do in the presence of outsiders. At home, he is protected from the rest of the world by the simple fact that he is surrounded by a family to whom he may turn for help, for sympathy, or for love.

When a youngster turns to his Home and his parents — who are the walking, talking embodiment of Home to him — it is very important that he be received with sympathy rather than criticism. Five-year-old Joey comes home in tears because he has fallen off his bike, cut his knee, and ripped his pants. His mother greets him with "Oh, Joey, look what you've done to your pants! You ought to be spanked!" He gets neither the sympathy nor the comfort that he expects, and if his mother reacts in this way frequently, Joey will become equally unfeeling about other people's misfortunes. She also passes up an opportunity to achieve a closeness and communication which arises only at a time of crisis — no matter how insignificant. Joey surely will not be as anxious to come to her the next time he is hurt as he would had she said, "Oh, Joey, let's see your knee. Come and let me wash it and put a Band-Aid on it." Then, having fixed him up and given him reasonable sympathy — in keeping with the seriousness of the wound — she is justified in mentioning her displeasure at his torn pants. In fact, she should not let her feeling sorry for him excuse his carelessness if the accident was avoidable. She has every right to show her displeasure. However, if he is just learning to ride, and she is allowing him to do so without supervision, she must expect accidents and be prepared to accept some damages. She may, in that case, show that she is sorry about the pants as well as his knee, but she has no right to be angry.

When Sally comes home from school with a bad report card, criticism and scolding will not encourage her to discuss her problems with you. Naturally you will show that you are not pleased — and Sally expects that. But she will also be far more disposed to try to improve her marks if you treat her sympathetically and take the positive approach of "I'm sorry this happened, Sally. Now, what can we do to help you improve the next report card?"

Scratched knees and bad report cards may seem far removed from manners, but how one deals with them is not. Once again, it is the matter of consideration which is important. If parents respect their children's feelings and treat their problems with sincerity the youngsters will tend to regard other people's problems in the same way. Thoughtfulness is born and nurtured at home, and it is another step in the child's development toward becoming a responsible, considerate adult.

Home, if a good rapport has been established, is the place where children will turn for advice. I firmly believe that youngsters should be encouraged to make their own decisions and to choose their own way of doing things whenever possible. But there are times when lack of knowledge or lack of experience makes it necessary for them to ask for help. And advice is far more valuable when it is sought after than when it is pushed on someone — child or adult. Unwanted "free" advice will not only go unheeded, but may even induce the listener to take the opposite course. If you feel that your child needs advice about something, but is reluctant to ask for it, by all means offer to try and help him out, but wait until your offer is accepted before dispensing your words of wisdom.

Home is the one place where you can prove to your children that living according to a code of consideration and unselfishness works; that it makes life more fun, as well as more meaningful. When the atmosphere surrounding a child is one of companionship, warmth, loyalty, and affection, that child is bound to grow up secure and self-confident. If the atmosphere is, instead, one of tension, rivalry, and each-man-for-himself, the value of having a home is entirely lost.

It's up to you. By your example, by your relationship as parents, and the feelings you manage to foster among all the members of your family, you will create the atmosphere that will influence your children all their lives. If they are lucky enough to grow up in the first atmosphere described, they will absorb those qualities themselves and will pass that heritage on to their children when they establish their own homes in their turn.

Even a very little child should be made to feel that his home *belongs* to him, and if he has brothers and sisters, to them, too. It is not only his parents' possession, but the whole family's. He is entitled to the joys of having a home — he must also be taught to assume the responsibilities.

Just as you start to teach a very small child to take care of his own things — to put his toys away when he is through with them, or to hang his clothes on hooks when he takes them off — you must go a step beyond and persuade him that his responsibility goes further. It extends to *family*-owned items as well. If he learns his lesson thoroughly, it will benefit him greatly later, because his sense of responsibility will extend to community property and he will become a valuable citizen whose concern goes far beyond his own backyard.

If you have not established the feeling that your home is shared — that it belongs to each child as well as to you, this will not work. His reaction will be, quite reasonably, "But that's yours, why should I have to take care of it?" To instill in him a sense of sharing your home, and pride in it, you must constantly display that attitude yourself. Forget "I" and "my" in talking about your home, and put in their places "we" and "our."

As your children grow beyond the infant stage, the success or failure of home life depends not only on you but on *every* member of the family. Each one must be persuaded and taught to cooperate and participate in all activities, chores as well as projects. As soon as they are able, youngsters should be taught that they can help by taking care of their own room. They then progress from this to taking part in chores which benefit the whole family — setting the table, raking leaves, or drying dishes. Too many parents in recent years have felt that children should not be made to share in such necessary daily jobs, but they are in error. How is a child to learn that one must *earn* one's rewards, if he is given all the pleasures of a comfortable home without lifting a finger to contribute to them? It involves the same type of responsibility discussed in the previous paragraph. By taking his part in the activities necessary to run a home, each member of the family develops a pride in the functioning of it, as well as the physical objects. He gets satisfaction out of the joint accomplishment, and the companionship of shared jobs helps promote family unity. But again, he must learn that if he does not participate in the "dirty work" (as well as the pleasanter chores) he will not be allowed to reap the benefits of that work. That is simply a matter of fairness to the other members of the family as well as a "lesson" to the laggard. The child who learns at home that he will be rewarded in proportion to the effort he puts in, will have a far easier adjustment to make later on.

To untold numbers of children, "Home" is synonymous with "Mother." She is the one who is always there, and gives the warmth, the security, and the love the child needs. But this is wrong — it should be "Mother *and* Dad." Every child needs masculine as well as feminine companionship, and no matter how good a parent a mom or a dad may be, it is not possible for her — or him — to provide both.

Little boys who are brought up in a home with no men around frequently become problems because they resent constantly taking orders from a woman. Women's Lib notwithstanding, boys are constantly exposed, through advertising, stories, and innumerable other ways, to the attitude that the man is the head of the family. He is pictured as the breadwinner, the decision-maker, the pillar of strength. Even though this is not necessarily true at all, it is the picture a little boy sees everywhere, and he identifies himself with that man. Therefore, when the person he is, by circumstance, forced to look to for decisions, for discipline, for advice, and so on, is a woman, it is not difficult to understand why he sometimes rebels. Boys need to feel a man's strength and be exposed to a masculine outlook on life, and the woman who is separated or divorced is wise if she makes every effort to see that he spends as much time as possible with men.

Uncles, grandfathers, or male friends with whom she is close enough to ask their assistance can help to substitute for a father although they can never replace him.

Girls, too, need the special sort of devotion which develops between a father and daughter. If a little girl has no brothers her father provides the only way in which she can learn to understand and appreciate male reactions and viewpoints. But a girl relates more closely to her mother, simply because they are of the same sex, has fewer of the resentments a boy may have, and therefore is less apt to get into trouble when brought up by a mother alone.

If both mother and father work and the child is left with a housekeeper or in a day-care center during the day, it is especially important that *both* parents devote a good many of their evening hours to making him feel that he has a Home. His physical comforts may be taken care of by someone else but his emotional security must be supplied by his mother and father's presence. Home is security and only a secure child is a happy one.

The Need for Privacy

In households where each child has his own room, the privacy of that room is inviolable. In general, doors are left open in homes where trust and companionship are present, but there are times in every child's life when he wants to be left alone. Even very young children may have this urge. Children are People, and even small People have rights and privileges which every other person in one household should respect. The right to privacy is one of the most important. It should never be susceptible to overthrow by older or more powerful members of the family. Your children should learn that their doors should never be locked, because this implies a distrust of other members of the household. In fact, the doors to very small children's rooms should not have keys or bolts that they can turn, because they are only too apt to lock themselves in and find they cannot unlock the door when they wish to. But a closed door, or one that is only slightly ajar, is a signal that the person inside wants to be alone — for whatever reason — and that wish should be respected. All that is required is that other members of the family learn to knock before opening the closed door, or ask, "May I come in?" The owner of the room will probably say, "Sure," but if he does not wish to see anyone at that moment, he has every *right* to say, "I'm sorry, I'm busy (or reading, or writing a letter) — come on in a little later."

Parents have the same right — their children should know that a closed door means "Don't come in without knocking." There are parents who feel that their door should never be closed to their children, but this is not so. They need not set a different standard for themselves from that set for their children, and they have every right to expect the same courtesy they give.

Mothers and fathers should never *lock* their doors, however, especially when their children are very young. A child who wakes up with a tummy-ache or a nightmare suffers a traumatic experience if he runs crying to his parents' room and finds the door locked.

When two children must share a room, their privacy is more difficult to preserve. In the case of young children, their mother must often help to satisfy the need by entertaining one child so that the other may be alone. As they grow older, their parents should help them work out a schedule which allows each to have the room to himself occasionally. This goes a long way toward lessening the inevitable arguments that arise between "roommates."

This all seems to indicate that I approve of closed doors. I don't — under ordinary circumstances, or most of the time. In the ideal home, every room is open and accessible to every member of the family — nine hours out of ten. But when the need for privacy occurs — and it does in almost everyone — every member of the family should be aware of and respect that need.

Eavesdropping

Parents have no more right to listen in on their child's conversation, than does the child on theirs. This is just as important a "privacy" as the right to be alone, and, again, is the privilege of every human being, child *or* adult. A cardinal rule in every household with more than one telephone is that any member who picks up the phone and hears someone talking must replace it immediately. It is the height of rudeness to listen to a conversation not intended for your ears.

The error is compounded if the offender then goes

and repeats what he has heard. If Frank accidentally overhears his sister Jennie's conversation with a friend, and reveals what he has heard, he breaks every rule of decency. If he keeps quiet or teases her when they are alone, that is another matter. As long as he doesn't deliberately listen longer than necessary, he and Jennie can settle the matter themselves and parents should not step in at all.

Sometimes parents are tempted to listen in on a youngster's conversation to find the answer to a question which has puzzled them, or the solution to a mystery such as "Who broke the cellar window?" This type of "spying" can only lead to trouble and distrust. Even our courts go to extremes to protect the rights of the individual against questionable forms of investigation, and if you employ those tactics at home, rather than relying on openness, you will destroy every bit of respect for law and decency your child may have developed. You will also destroy his faith in *you*, because at the same time you are revealing your distrust in him. To keep your own decency and dignity intact, and to promote those qualities in your child, you must never undermine his confidence in you — or his innate honesty — by spying.

Letters and Diaries

The right of any individual to keep his letters and his diary as secret as he wishes is inviolable. Even husbands and wives must respect that right, and many a marriage has been shaken because one member could not resist the temptation to see from whom that strange letter came.

One of the greatest delights your youngster can have is to receive a letter addressed to HIM or to HER! He has watched you open your mail for a long time and now it is *his* turn. Can you imagine his disappointment if you say, "Why, here's a letter for you, Tommy; I'll open it for you." Tommy may be so small that he cannot read his letter, but don't just take it upon yourself to do so. *Ask* him first if he would like to have you read it to him. You will make him feel "grown up" by giving him the choice, and his pleasure in his first letter will be doubled. If he is old enough to read it himself — or almost by himself — don't even suggest that you give any help, unless he requests it.

Later, when your child will receive "business" letters

from his school, stores, and so on, the same rule holds true. Unless he asks that you open the mail which is obviously not personal, you should hold it until he can open it himself, or forward it to him.

The same "home-rights rule" holds true for packages. Surely one of the best parts of receiving a gift is opening it. When Billy's birthday present from Grandmother arrives in the mail, make a ceremony of the opening. Shake it, discuss it, try to guess what it is. As the anticipation builds, so will his pleasure. Then, give him the necessary tools (cut the string or tape for him if he is very small) and let him take off the wrapping paper and open the box — BY HIMSELF.

Some children start to keep a diary of sorts when they are very small — as soon as they can write. This, too, should be their *own* and no one has a right to read it unless asked to. A child who can put down his private thoughts and opinions in even the most elementary way has a valuable outlet or "release valve," and the urge should be encouraged. Furthermore, it is a wonderful early step in learning to express himself. But he must be made to feel that it is only for his own pleasure — if he wishes it that way — and that there is no danger that putting his secret thoughts on paper will result in revelations he does not want to make to other people.

Just as is true of eavesdropping, the contents of letters and diaries should *never* be used to prove or disprove an accusation, or solve a mystery. Unless, of course, the writer grants permission. Otherwise, they are the most private possessions a person can have, and should be treated as such.

The Right to Relax

Overworked as the expression "All work and no play make Jack a dull boy" may be, there is more truth than fiction in it, and the harder a youngster works, the more he needs to play. Work takes many forms — studying, doing household chores, or for very young children, merely learning — but the difference between work and play is that work is always something that is required, whereas play is something one can do or not, as he wishes. Parents should strive to strike a balance between the two. A surfeit of one is as disastrous as a lack of the other.

The most important element of relaxation is doing what one wants to do. If it is silly or meaningless, that's all right. If it is restful or educational, so much the better. But a child's impulse to make up foolish games for himself, or to talk to imaginary characters, or to draw unrealistic pictures should not be discouraged. The only time that his diversion should be rechanneled or brought to a halt is when it might be harmful to himself, or to someone else. You, as a parent, may, of course, encourage your youngster to put his relaxing time to good use by suggesting that he read or look at worthwhile books in place of an endless flow of comic books, or suggesting that he watch some TV shows that are to some extent educational rather than only cartoons or Westerns. But you should never put it on the basis of, "Watch 'Sesame Street,' or don't watch at all."

Parents who are talented in a special field are apt to be the worst offenders in this area. A concert pianist or an opera singer, if she sees the faintest hint of those talents in her child, may ruin his life by trying to push him into the same career. The minute he sits down and picks up a book, she is after him. "Why aren't you practicing? Why are you wasting your time?" From the time they get up in the morning until they close their eyes at night these children are nagged at to study, to practice, to perform, to the exclusion of all other interests. A very small minority will, perhaps, follow the pattern and become successful. The vast majority will rebel. They will end up dead set against playing the piano — or against music of any kind. An avocation which they might naturally have picked up from their mother and enjoyed to the full as a hobby or an art, if not a career, has been completely denied them because of enforced participation.

This is true of many fields other than the arts. The father who waits for his son to mature only so that he may follow in his footsteps by going to a certain college and then into the world of finance or medicine, is due for a shattering disappointment. The mother who went to Smith and loved every minute has no reason to enroll her daughter the day she is born. The girl may not be college material at all, or she may want to go west, or north, or south — and that should be her prerogative. To insist that she work and struggle to achieve something because you did, is depriving her of her right to find her own niche, and to relax, mentally as well as physically.

Many of the youngsters who rebel against their parents — even to the extent of running away from home (total rejection), do so because they have been "pushed." Whether openly or subtly their parents have been nagging at them: "Why can't you get marks like Sammy Conklin's?" "How do you expect to get anyplace if you don't work?" "Aren't you ashamed to bring home a report card like that?" and so on and so on. The child, especially if he has respect for his parents and wants to please them, is driven harder and harder, often beyond his capacity. Then, of course, something snaps. When the realization comes that, no matter how hard he tries, he *can't* do what is expected of him, he gives up. He quits, or he actively rebels by leaving home, by becoming totally antisocial, or by turning to a crutch such as drugs.

Today, where demands on children are more trying than they have ever been, and pressures more over-powering, the time to relax — to do nothing, if you wish — is more important than ever. If you want your child to withstand the strain, encourage his foolish-ness, his occasional idleness, and his desire for just plain fun. Join him — be silly with him, laugh with him, rest with him. It will do both of you good. The unfinished chore may prove more valuable than the job which was completed against all odds, leaving the worker exhausted. But one word of warning: Every job must be completed eventually. One of the most dangerous habits your child can develop is that of not finishing what he starts. It should be completed, how-ever, without undue strain — the work periods inter-spersed with hours of rest or play, so that when the

job is accomplished, he is ready and able to enjoy —
not resent — the fruits of his labor.

Running Errands

There are some parents who seem to feel that their
children were put into this world only to be their
personal servants. They apparently believe that their
youngsters have nothing to do but run errands for
them.

"Sally, run upstairs and get my glasses for me."
"Chuck, would you see if I left my knitting on the
porch?" "Ellie, take this book over to Mrs. Sibley's,
will you?" It makes no difference whether Ellie was
watching her favorite TV shows, or Chuck was building a birdhouse, or Sally was coloring a picture for
her homework. They must, unless they want to provoke an argument or a punishment — and this is exactly what eventually happens — drop whatever they
are doing and act as Mother's "errand boy."

Don't let yourself fall into this habit. Try and put
yourself in Sally's position. If *she* asked *you* to help
her with her homework in the middle of *your* favorite

show, wouldn't you say, "I'll be there as soon as this show is over, Sally." Sally should surely have the *right* to respond in the same way.

There are, of course, situations which merit an instant response. If you are in your bathrobe and slippers and your husband goes out to the garage to drive to work, leaving his briefcase behind, you are certainly justified in calling, "Hank, hurry, take this briefcase to Dad before he gets off without it!" — no matter what Hank is doing at the moment.

In general, the more important the occupation of the child, the more important that he be allowed to pursue it uninterrupted. Of course, what may seem unimportant to you may be a matter of vital concern to him. Your little girl might, for example, be playing quietly with her doll when you ask her to bring in the evening paper. "Wait until I get Jane into bed, Mommy, she's saying her prayers." This imaginative play may not seem so important to you, but it *is* to your daughter. She would expect you to make the same reply if someone called you on the telephone or Dad asked her to look for his slippers while you were in the middle of hearing *her* prayers.

If, on the other hand, she is simply sitting around killing time, or doing something which can be put down and picked up again, you have every right to ask her to do an errand for you at any time. This is your privilege, and every child should learn to expect such requests, just as he soon learns to make them of you. It is part of the give-and-take that should be normal in every family. In fact, because a youngster is younger and has more energy than his parents, he should be expected to do more than his share. And he will, if you are fair about choosing the right time to ask for his help, and keeping the number of requests within reason.

"Instant" Obedience

If your husband were in the middle of a magazine article when you called, "Dinner's ready," and he didn't come *at once*, would you snatch the magazine away from him and put it back in the rack? Of course you wouldn't! And yet that, in effect, is what many parents do to their children. Let us say that your son, Jimmy, has two more blocks left to complete his tower, so he delays a minute or two to finish it before minding your "Come this minute and wash your hands." Annoyed, you take him by the arm and haul him to his feet, knocking his castle helter-skelter in the process. He starts to cry; you, because you feel guilty, lash out at him, and the dinner hour is ruined for everyone. How much better it would have been if you had told him five minutes ahead of time that he had just that long to finish his building. A second, two-minute warning would have served to remind him, and still give him time to finish his project. As in the case of running errands, you have every right to expect obedience — and prompt obedience — but not at all costs. Furthermore, by demanding that he leave whatever he is doing regardless of the situation (if, for example, he were gluing something and the glue would dry too much if left until after dinner), you are encouraging a very bad habit — that of leaving a job unfinished. By dragging the youngster away abruptly, interrupting his train of thought as well as the physical process, he may lose interest and find it difficult to go back to where he left off. If you can devise a system which will help him to organize his projects so that they may be put aside and started again in a reasonable way, you will be doing him a great service. The best suggestion I can make is to decide upon a "warning" time, or "put-away" time that will give him the necessary leeway to finish what he is doing and to pick up his implements or toys. This time limit can apply in all situations and if it is agreed upon between you, it is up to you to see that both you and your child abide by it. Don't "cheat" on your warning time, and insist that he honor your agreement, too.

Your Child and His Possessions

A sense of possession is one of the most primitive instincts. In its most elemental form, a possession is something to guard — to fight for or to hide from others. In its higher expression it is something to cherish — to care for and love. One of the first lessons a child must learn about possessions is the difference between "his" and "not his."

You must encourage him to develop at the earliest possible age, *respect* for the possessions of others, and *responsibility* for his own. Other members of his family (and later, outsiders) have the same right to do as they wish with their possessions as he has with his. To try to destroy your child's possessive instincts by ridiculing them, or by not showing due respect for his things, will not only create antagonism, but may change his inclination from one of protector to one of destroyer.

Children who have been granted the most freedom in their choice of and care of their own treasures are the children who show the most consideration for the property of others. Their parents have always honored their right to collect and care for anything they wish (as long as it is harmless, of course). If it is something of value to their child, mother and father treat it as something of value to them, too. When Katie comes home with her pocket full of dusty white pebbles for her collection, her mother carefully puts them on Katie's table before putting the bluejeans in the laundry. She treats the pebbles just as carefully as she expects Katie to treat her collection of china match boxes, because — for the moment — the pebbles mean just as much to Katie as does the more valuable china to her.

It is not usually difficult to convince your young child that his toys depend on him to keep them from being hurt or broken. This is especially true when the toy is a doll or an animal which is, in his eyes, very real. Most children are sensitive, and in addition to the fact that they can *see* that their toy loses its beauty, its usefulness, or its ability to entertain them, they often, when they are very small, believe that inanimate objects actually feel pain. On the other hand, if you make too much of an issue of it when your youngster breaks or maltreats his toys, you may find him methodically damaging everything he owns — simply to get the added attention from you. Far better than scolding him when he breaks anything, is an effort to stimulate his interest in fixing it. You achieve two ends if you can succeed in teaching him to mend the damage if it is possible: One, the lesson in dexterity, ingenuity, or whatever the repair requires, and two, instilling in him a *constructive* impulse. A child who spends time and effort in fixing or beautifying something is not apt to want to destroy it. When your youngster pries open his Mickey Mouse watch, to see what makes it tick, or unscrews the bolts holding his toy car together to find out what makes it go, he is not being destructive. He is merely displaying a healthy curiosity which should be commended rather than discouraged. However, he should also be encouraged and taught to put the object back together again.

Wanton destruction is another matter entirely, and requires much firmer handling. It is essential that you check the more violent impulses in your child, or he may well grow up to indulge in the vandalism we see so much of today. By your firm disapproval of his carelessness or destructiveness, and by your choice of methods of correction, you can help him to recognize the futility of such behavior. When Mickey took a hammer and smashed his toy wagon to bits, simply because he enjoyed the noise and the violence of the action, his mother showed great restraint. She did not scold or lecture him other than to point out that it was too bad he would no longer have a cart to play with because of his own thoughtless action. She quietly removed the remains and firmly refused to listen to his apologies and requests for a new cart. Had she given in to Mickey or in to her own irritation by allowing herself to become angry and making a real crisis of it, he would have been intrigued with the attention and the importance placed on his misdeed. He might well have gone on to other destruction, enjoying both the act and the result.

When a child deliberately breaks other people's possessions, it becomes serious enough so that, if reasoning fails, punishment of some sort is necessary. One very effective method of discouraging such behavior is punishment in kind. Again it is very important for Mother, or for the owner of the damaged object, to avoid a display of temper. Neither lecturing nor physical punishment such as spanking is generally effective in this situation.

Melissa, aged four, having always seemed a sweet

and tractable child, suddenly started scribbling over everything she could find; books, magazines, letters — even the furniture. Her mother hid her crayons. Melissa brought others home from school. Her mother pleaded, scolded, and threatened. Melissa happily, if more furtively, scribbled on. Finally, her mother decided to take drastic action. She scrawled over many of Melissa's favorite possessions (using chalk, which could be easily wiped off) — her books, her blackboard, and her coloring set. When Melissa came home from nursery school she took one look at her room and burst into tears. "Clean it up, Mommy, clean it up." "No, Melissa," replied her mother. "Since you went right on destroying my things, I have a right to destroy yours." After some further discussion about "property rights" they came to an agreement. They each helped the other clean off the chalk and the crayon marks. Melissa promised to keep her scribbling to her own pads and coloring books, and her mother promised her a new set of coloring materials — as long as they were to be properly used. By resorting to "punishment in kind," Melissa's mother taught her daughter a valuable lesson in the futility of destructiveness.

Your example is of prime importance in teaching your youngster responsibility for his belongings. If you let your furniture get broken and don't have it fixed, if you leave tools outdoors to be ruined by rain, or stolen, if you don't put your playing cards away in their boxes, or books back on the shelves to keep them clean and undamaged, how can you expect your child to pay much attention when you tell him to take care of *his* things? Only if you show your respect for your possessions can you expect your children to do the same.

Mr. Barton came home from work one day and found the tools from his workshop and an assortment of odd pieces of lumber lying in the driveway. He called his five-year-old son from the house and asked the meaning of this. Bobby explained he was trying to make a doghouse for his pet but found he couldn't get the nails in straight enough so he had given up. Mr. Barton showed great restraint. Instead of "blowing up" and punishing Bobby, he realized that he had never thought to *teach* him about proper care and use of tools. He sat down with Bobby, explained how the tools could be harmed by misuse and lack of care, and promised to buy him some appropriate to his size. They agreed that Bobby would be completely responsible for them, would not use his father's without permission, and would not ask for replacements if he lost or broke any tool through carelessness. Mr. Barton's good sense and restraint turned what could have been an unhappy experience into a valuable lesson — and he and his son took a step toward real companionship. The whole incident need never have taken place, however, had Mr. Barton insisted, when Bobby was younger, that he take proper care of tools, and had he set a good enough example himself.

Your Children's Friends

Devoted parents of a small child sometimes feel some pangs of jealousy as their youngster matures. The baby who has been completely dependent on them for all his happiness, suddenly starts to look for some of it elsewhere. Even very young children are attracted to people of their own size and interests and this tendency begins almost as soon as they are old enough to communicate intelligibly. As they grow, the urge to form friendships should be encouraged. No intelligent parent would want it otherwise, because it is all part of the child's training in independence, in development of good judgments, and in loyalty.

It does not mean that family devotion ends — it is merely an additional dimension in the child's relationships. If the family ties are secure, they are not shaken. They keep their own place in the child's heart but they no longer have the *only* place.

Parents who are jealous of the outside friendships, interests, and, finally, loves, of their child will quickly lose their own place in his affection. The mother who is jealous of her youngster's admiration for her teacher, or the father who tries to dominate his son's life entirely are only losing ground in the struggle to retain their child's affection. No human being can monopolize another, no matter what the relationship, and the sooner you, as a parent, realize that your child will want and need outside interests and ties, the sooner you will see the advantages to both of you. A truly devoted parent recognizes from the start the importance of the child's ability to make friends, and to take an interest in people, outside of the family. A youngster's making a first friend is a great step forward, which should be greeted not with resentment, but with joy and enthusiasm.

Human beings are by nature gregarious. You must be prepared for the time when your baby will become a member of a group. Most of his impulses for some time will stem from a desire to conform to that group — to emulate the older or stronger members and to win the approval of all of them. During this period you can support him by accepting his friends, and you can also help him develop judgment and discrimination by tactfully — not critically — letting him know which playmates are most worthy of his friendship — and why. It is important that you do not show open dislike for one or the other. The effect will be exactly the reverse of what you want. His instinct will be to fly to the other child's defense, and by doing so he will tend to become more, rather than less, interested in and attracted to the other.

If your attitude toward your Marian's little friends is warm and welcoming, they will feel it, as well as Marian. Your house will soon become the meeting place, and you will be among the most fortunate of parents. Marian's friend Judy's parents wonder why their home is not the center of activity with its swimming pool and playground area. Or little John's mother cannot understand why he is constantly at someone else's house when she serves such delicious snacks to his friends. The answer is simple — there is no warmth or welcome in either house. In Judy's, the children are confined to the play area, and constantly reminded not to dirty this, damage that, and so on. John's mother is making an effort, but she is trying too hard to buy the group's affection by bribery. Neither John's nor Judy's mother has the ability to put the gang at ease through genuine liking and interest.

Children flock to the house where they are allowed to play as they wish. This does not mean there should be no rules — small children actually prefer the security of knowing that someone has said, "You may do this" or "You may not do that." But once the regulations have been explained to them carefully and clearly, it should be assumed that they will adhere to them without constant "policing." When a mother *believes* that her child and his playmates will be "good," they generally react by being "good."

Youngsters need and love to make noise. And, unless you live in an apartment where others would be disturbed, they should be allowed to do so. If you have a headache or need peace and quiet that day you have every right to ask the gang to play elsewhere. But if you invite them in, don't ruin the happy image of your hospitality by insisting that they cater to your indisposition.

No matter how well-meaning and how well-behaved a group of children generally is, they can quickly get out of hand if excitement and warfare are allowed to go unchecked. For this reason, it is *very* important that an adult is always nearby when a group of little children gathers. Not long ago four or five little boys of kindergarten age were playing in my neighbor's game room. They started throwing Ping-Pong balls at each other — a harmless enough sport. But one thing led to another, tempers began to flare, and all of a sudden they were throwing the billiard balls instead! My neighbor put a stop to it when she heard the crashing from the third floor, but not before there was a toll of one broken ashtray, one cracked window, a smashed finger, and two bloody noses. You can't always be right on hand when trouble starts, but this is a good example of why it is important that you are at least nearby.

Whether your home is large or small or lavish or simple makes little difference to your children's friends. Space helps, of course, and so do games and play equipment. But the atmosphere is what really counts. The mother who realizes that and works to create a welcoming air is repaid many times over in seeing her child surrounded by friends, and by rarely having to ask, "I wonder where Billy and the other kids are today."

A youngster must be taught very early that he has certain responsibilities in regard to his friends. If Billy asks Chuck over to play the following day, he must remember it, and he must be there when Chuck arrives. He must not go off with Howie, who comes by and says, "Let's go over to the school yard and climb on the bars." If Billy isn't home when Chuck arrives, Chuck is going to hesitate before he agrees to come over again. It is simply a matter of consideration. If you have constantly reminded Billy to think of the other fellow, he will understand when you say, "How would *you* have felt if Chuck asked you over and wasn't home when you got there?" Encouraging him to look at it from the other's point of view will help him to act more considerately and to understand how thoughtlessness can hurt, and can also backfire in resulting unpopularity.

Billy should also learn to share his toys and possessions with the children he plays with. If he persists (after you have talked to him about sharing) in being stingy and hanging on to the best toys himself, send his friends home. Explain to him that he is hurting himself as well as making them unhappy. They will not like him if he acts that way, and it is better that they don't come over to play until he agrees to be generous and fair with them. Furthermore, you must impress on him that he has to take care of and return promptly the toys that other children share with him. When he is hungry or thirsty, he should be taught that it is only hospitable to offer food and drink to his playmates. If there is not enough cake to go around, don't give it to him alone. Find a substitute, or simply say, "Sorry, fellows, there just isn't enough to go around, and it wouldn't be fair to give it to some of you and not the others."

While you are teaching your youngster the duties of a host or hostess, you may come up against a slightly different problem. What are his obligations if the situation is not of his making?

Here is a letter I received recently:

Dear Mrs. Post:

My daughter is five years old. When my friend comes to visit me, and brings her four-year-old, must my Holly entertain this child for as long as she is our guest? If Trudy doesn't want to play with Holly's "gang," must Holly be kept from her friends, too?

The problem is to arrive at a compromise between teaching Holly the responsibilities of a hostess, and not forcing on her a course of action resulting from something which was not of her own choosing. Since Mrs. X. arranged the visit for her own pleasure, it is really not fair to expect Holly to give up the entire afternoon or to play something which may not be to her liking. At the same time, you should insist that she help you out — as "co-hostess" — by greeting the child (and her mother) and inviting her to join in the neighborhood activities. If Trudy refuses, Holly should bring out some of her toys until she finds something that will keep Trudy happy. Then, after playing with the guest for a little while, Holly may go to join her friends. After a time, call her in to play for another short time, or help you serve refreshments.

If you do not insist on her giving up her entire playtime in your interests, and if you discuss the situation thoroughly with her ahead of time, she will learn to look forward to — or at least tolerate — visits from strangers, rather than considering them a bore and an imposition.

There are very few formal manners that need be observed among very young friends. However, you can help your child achieve more popularity and better relationships if certain good manners are so firmly instilled in him that it is natural for him to use them with his friends as well as with you or with your contemporaries.

Greetings

"Hi" or "Hi, Jimmy" said with warmth, is all that is necessary. The important thing is that after any separation — a day or a week or a month — friends show their pleasure in seeing each other by an instant and enthusiastic greeting and response. You can help your child to realize this by your cheerful "Good morning" when you wake him, and your smiling "Hi," or "Hello, Tommy" when you pick him up after school. It isn't hard to suggest that he reply with "Hi, Mom," but haven't you seen children who respond with a mere grunt, or not at all? Surely the effect would be as dampening to one of his own age. But if you make friendly greetings a habit in your home, among your family members, and if you insist on polite "hellos" with your friends, it will become quite natural to him to greet his own friends in the same way.

Introductions

Preschool children are certainly not ready to perform formal introductions, but they can start to learn the value and the object of introductions at a very early age. You can help to make this often-awkward social gesture easier by being very careful to introduce your child to strangers — naturally and properly — whenever the occasion arises. When you take him shopping and run into your old schoolmate you haven't seen for years, don't leave him standing unnoticed

until, perhaps, your friend says, "Is this your oldest
— what's his name?" Instead, after greeting her, say,
"And I want you to meet our oldest son, Karl. Karl,
this is Mrs. Gordon. I went to school with her." Your
youngster is not about to introduce his friends in that
way, of course, but if you make a point of doing it
regularly, he will unconsciously absorb the knowledge
that an introduction makes one feel "included" and
comfortable. As he matures, you should teach him the
simple basic rules so that they will come naturally to
him later. He will start simply by saying, "Johnny, this
is Bobby" and progress from there to the more complicated forms involving adults. Training in introductions can actually be started when your child is only
three or so by making a game of it. When he comes
into the kitchen carrying his Teddy bear, you might
exclaim, "Why, who is that nice-looking bear with you,
Peter? Won't you introduce us?" He'll probably say
something like "Oh, don't be silly, you know this old
bear, Mommy." This is your chance to explain how
people like to be introduced so they won't feel left out,
and how it helps when you know the names of people
you meet. Perhaps Bear will feel very grown up if
Peter says, "Why, this is Mr. Bear, Mommy" and you
can go on with, "How nice to meet you, Mr. Bear." If
you have a little girl, you will have even more oppor-

tunity to play this sort of game with her dolls. In fact, your children's animals and dolls provide a wonderful "third person" for you to use as an example in teaching many manners.

When he is about to face a situation in which he will meet new friends — his first day at school, or when you move to a new community or go to a summer resort, for instance — you can help him over the hump and start him on the right track by preparing him in advance to introduce himself. Explain that everyone will want to know his name, but they may be too shy or not know how to ask. Therefore he can help by saying, "I'm Sonny. What's your name?" Practice this with him, making up silly games if you wish, to keep the game from becoming boring. If you do it frequently, the reluctance to focus attention on himself, and to be the one to make the first gesture of friendship by saying, "I'm Sonny" will be greatly minimized.

Until he is in grade school, however, he only needs to learn two simple rules. Men are introduced *to* women, and younger people are introduced *to* older people. This is accomplished by the simple expedient of saying the woman's or the older person's name first: "Mary, this is Henry," or "Mrs. Smith, I'd like you to meet Mr. Jones"; "Mr. Howard, this is my friend Jamie," or "Aunt Susan, I'd like you to meet Sally, my new neighbor." As soon as your child is old enough to remember, he should include the word of explanation, "My friend, my neighbor," and so on.

Please and thank you

I would like to point out here that you will be doing your child a favor if you remind him frequently that "please" and "thank you" are as pleasant to hear at four as at forty. Everyone likes to be appreciated, and what better way can one express appreciation than by saying thank you? And even a very unpopular request is made more palatable if it is followed by please.

There is one essential requirement in teaching your youngsters to say please and thank you, and that is to say them yourself. There are too many parents who invariably insist that their child say please when he asks for anything, but constantly say to him, "Do thus and so" or "Hand me that" without so much as a "would you?" let alone a "please." No matter how often they insist, it will never take hold because their child, sooner or later, will rebel at the authoritative attitude they reveal. "Please" is the word that changes an order to a request, and who doesn't prefer that to being "bossed"? It implies that the speaker respects the person he is speaking to, and considers him an equal. Harsh, abrupt commands — "Get up," "Come here," "Do this," "Do that," and so on, have a definite master-servant ring. And that, I hope, is not the relationship you wish to create between yourself and your youngster.

Your two-year-old, naturally, is not going to remember his "pleases" all the time, simply because you do. It will be some years before it comes naturally to him. In the meantime it is up to you to remind him constantly. When he is very small you will have to ask, "What do you say?" or "How do you ask?" when he says "I want a cookie." As he gets a little older you need only ignore his requests — pointedly — until he adds please. Point out to him that it is a magic word; that not only will people like him better, but he will get what he wants much faster and much more often when he uses it. But be sure he knows that the satisfaction is not only a selfish one; the use of please also shows his respect and consideration for the people around him.

Occasionally small children who are learning to talk, and are experimenting with how far they can go and what they can get away with, become very aggressive and demanding. They are trying to exert their authority, and they go through a stage of "I want that *now*" or "Gimme it." Firmness, calmness, and a sense of humor are necessary to see you through such a period. Refuse, at all costs, to give in to those demands. Say, "Not until you say please," and stick with it. If he grabs for the object, grab it back. If he slaps, as I have seen youngsters do, slap him back. Never in the face, and with restraint of course, so that he gets no more than a good sting, but enough to show him you mean business. If he is as stubborn as most children, he will not give in and say please this time, but he will be more apt to remember the next or the next.

This lesson in please should be one of the highest on your list of important manners, because it is one of the ones, if not *the* one, which will do him the most good for the rest of his life.

Thank you is as important as please in its own way, but the use, or lack of use, of it has a less immediate and less obvious result. Thank you is simply a matter of showing appreciation, and it should come from the heart. It results in making the person who says it well-liked and it leads his associates to want to do more for him. But like please, it is not only a selfish motive for which you teach your child to say thank you. It is also because each time he says it, he is developing a habit of consideration, of thought for another person's feelings. Ingratitude, or the lack of ability to show your gratitude, is the sign of either a very selfish or a very inhibited person.

You cannot teach your child to use thank you as you do please because the request is already granted or the gift already given. So you must rely more heavily on your own example, combined with frequent reminders and explanations of the value of the word and thought.

5

Everyday Manners

WHEN GOOD MANNERS come to be a natural part of a person, so natural that he does not even think about whether he is doing things right or not, he can face any situation with perfect self-confidence. A friend of mine was unexpectedly presented to Queen Elizabeth during a trip to England last summer. When she came home, her friends wanted to know how she had known what to do, and "hadn't she been scared to death?" "Not at all," she said. "It was very simple. I only *have* one set of manners." This sort of composure is a gift well worth giving your youngster. And he will develop it if you insist that he learn the rudiments of good manners both in your home and outside it.

Of course you and your children are less formal at home, and you rightfully omit some of the formalities you might use in public. But basically, *your* home manners must be just as sound as your company manners. After all, it is at home that your children will learn their manners and it is *your* example which will teach them. It is also at home, where the family is constantly "on top of" each other, that manners assume the greatest importance. If every member does not learn to cooperate and to treat each other with consideration, life at home becomes a disaster. You cannot escape from each other as you do from the friends you only see at times, and constant contact requires even more restraint — and effort — than less intimate association.

Whether in your house or out of it, there are some general rules which your youngsters must follow. These are plain, everyday, common-sense good manners, and were they not observed, our society and our relationships with each other would soon deteriorate into a sort of social anarchy.

Too many parents simply do not realize that these things must be taught. They seem to assume that they will be assimilated by a mysterious process of osmosis, or that teachers or other youngsters will instill the rules in their children. Or, if they do think about it, many think that rules of courtesy are too strict or too confining for the easygoing and tolerant attitude of today. That is not so. The mode of behavior which we accept as "good manners" is merely a guideline, designed to make life pleasanter for everyone. Once your child has been exposed to the rules, he may adhere to (or discard) those he thinks are important (or worthless) as his experience grows. Most manners may be interpreted as strictly or as loosely as you think fit. For example, one family may follow the "respect older people rule" by insisting that little Karen curtsy every time she is introduced to an adult. Other parents may feel that a friendly handshake is sufficient. Either way is perfectly "correct." Those rules which are restrictive are only so because if not obeyed, they result in harm to others or to the child himself.

Orderliness

One cannot live successfully within the limits of acceptable behavior without orderliness. Good grooming, neatness, and promptness help, first, to develop self-respect. Second, they demonstrate that one is concerned about the effect he has on his community — whether it be a two-room apartment for a family of three, or a city of 100,000 people. Your baby's community is closer to the two-room apartment, but orderliness is just as important there (or more so, because of the limited facilities) as it is in the twenty-room mansion of a rich executive.

Good Grooming

Little girls have less innate resistance to soap and water than little boys, but it is important to teach both the necessity for cleanliness. As soon as your baby is ready to sit up in a high chair and eat regular food (other than milk from bottles) you should start washing his hands before each meal. Never tell him he *surely will* get sick if he doesn't wash — because he probably won't — but as soon as he is able to understand, you can discuss how dirt increases his *chances* of catching an illness. Furthermore, you can point out how unpleasant sticky or greasy hands *feel*. As he gets old enough to wash up himself, constant reminders will be necessary. But try to avoid repetitious nagging and devise ways to encourage and praise instead. Children, like adults, enjoy compliments, and if you dwell on the happy results of washing rather than scolding and criticizing, the chore will seem far more worthwhile.

I've never heard of a baby who didn't love his bath as soon as he became accustomed to the feel of the water. Provided, of course, that his mother regarded bathtime as a pleasure and an extension of playtime.

Allow plenty of time for your child's bath and let him "swim," play with toys, and enjoy it to the full. Nothing can do more to instill in him a feeling that cleanliness is something desirable, and that regular bathing can be fun — not just a necessity.

As soon as your youngster wants to take her brush or comb in her own hand, let her try it. You will undoubtedly catch your little daughter — at a very early age — trying to comb or braid her doll's hair. Encourage her and show her how — even if she seems to be pulling the wig right off. Let her know that you think it's great that she cares about Mehitabel's appearance — *just as you care about hers.* Try to choose a hair style for her which will stay neat without constant fussing. If you like her hair long, tie it back with an Alice-in-Wonderland ribbon. Or try a ponytail or braids. If her hair is curly, or you like a pixie look, cut it short. But she will be far more receptive to learning to care for her hair and keep it neat if it does not require perpetual combing, brushing, and rearranging.

Boys are less concerned about their appearance than girls, but fathers can help tremendously by inviting their sons in to keep them company while they shave, letting them share their shower from time to time, and admiring a new shirt, or praising their neatly combed hair or clean fingernails.

The evening meal, as the main family "social" event of the day, is the time to insist that good personal habits are formed. Make it clear to your children that they must come to the table with washed hands, combed hair, and reasonably clean, neat clothing or they will be excused to eat by themselves. Impress on them that no one individual has the right to spoil the occasion for the others, as the presence of a sloppy, dirty diner can easily do.

One method of instilling an interest in clothing and appearance in your youngster is to let him share with you the fun of choosing his own clothes. Take him with you to shop whenever it is possible. If you simply go and select his clothes for him there will be no opportunity for him to learn to discriminate — to choose between this or that — or to develop a sense of what is sensible, practical and attractive for him. Girls will appreciate this opportunity more than boys, perhaps, but the boys, too, can be encouraged to take an interest in choosing the right clothing. You must, of course, direct and guide their taste, but insofar as it is feasible, go along with their choices.

Don't force clothes on your youngster which make him feel silly or "different." My husband still remembers with loathing the day when he was sent to school in an Eton suit with short pants, while the other boys wore long flannel trousers. Don't go for the ultra "cute" clothes, or for adult styles cut down to a child's size. It may seem entertaining to you to choose identical mother-and-daughter sets — and to be sure, if the style is simple and right, they *can* be fun — but be careful that they do not merely make your child look like a caricature of an adult.

Neatness

I am convinced that most children, no matter how immaculate the surroundings they grow up in, are not naturally neat. Boys who grew up with nurses continually picking up after them are no neater as men than others who lived in a pigsty. Girls whose mothers never left a fleck of dust on a table or a dish unwashed in the sink develop with no apparent urge to hang up or put away even their most beloved clothing. Good example, in this case, is simply not enough.

There are people, children included, who *are* naturally neat. It distresses them to see things out of place, and in some cases this is such a compelling force, that they drive themselves, and everyone about them, crazy. I have a friend who has two college-age daughters, only a year apart and brought up in exactly the same way. One is immaculate in her appearance but must be constantly reminded to make her bed, hang up her clothes, and so on. The other is exactly the opposite. Clothes and makeup mean very little to her, but her room and possessions are always in perfect order.

You, as a parent, will find it a real challenge to instill an appreciation of all-over orderliness in your child. Example, while not the answer, is, of course, necessary. The youngster who sees that his parents consider neat surroundings desirable and important will inevitably be more interested in the attractiveness of his home than the one whose parents don't care themselves.

If you expect your child to make the effort to take care of his things and to put them away, you must start, when he is between two and three, by making it as easy as possible. It is essential that he has a *place* to put things, and that you patiently and persistently insist that he put them in that place. Clothes hooks in his closet at his own eye level make it possible for him to hang up his clothes himself. The rail for the clothes that require hangers should be lowered to where he can easily reach it. A receptacle for dirty clothes *in his room* — not down the hall in the bathroom — will encourage him to put them where they belong. Toyboxes for blocks and nonbreakables, shelves for more perishable toys, and drawers and boxes for small items such as crayons and marbles are necessities. With ingenuity, and the availability of ready-made (even cardboard) chests, bins, boxes, and so on, even the smallest room can provide a great deal of storage space.

Once you have provided him with the facilities for keeping his own room neat, and shown him how to use them, the only thing you can do is remind him, encourage him, and praise him when he does well. Even though his progress in keeping his own room in order is negligible or slow, you must accept the fact that in that area, he is hurting no one but himself. If it is more than you can bear, you can simply shut his door so that you and the rest of the family need not look at his "mess." Do not let yourself become so upset by his laziness that you break down and straighten up for him. That is just what he is hoping you will do. It may become a contest of wills — don't lose it. Don't make a crisis of it either, by losing your temper. He will get an equal amount of satisfaction from the excitement and attention. As long as his messiness is not hurting the rest of the family, let him suffer the *natural* consequences. They may prove to be the best teacher of all.

Helen, four years old, looked forward tremendously to going to her grandmother's for Sunday dinner every week, and enjoyed getting dressed in clean "best" clothes for the occasion.

For some time, Helen's mother had been trying to teach Helen to hang up and put away her clothes. She discussed the situation with a friend who had older children and received a valuable suggestion. The next week, after the Sunday outing, Helen, as usual, flung her clothes all over the floor. This time, much to Helen's surprise, her mother neither nagged, punished, nor picked them up. She left them where they were, along with the everyday clothes that received the same treatment. On Friday, Helen couldn't find a clean blouse for nursery school, since her blouses were still lying on the floor. Her mother merely suggested that she find one that wasn't *too* rumpled, so that it would do for school. Sunday came, and Helen asked what she would wear, since her good clothes were not hanging in her closet. Her mother explained that since Helen was expected to be dressed in her best, and clean and neat at her grandmother's, she was not going to be able to go. She repeated, for at least the tenth time, why it was important to put clothes in the laundry hamper, or hang them up. She reminded Helen that she had constantly warned her of the results if she did not take care of her things. So, on Sunday, with no display of anger and no argument — on her mother's part — Helen was left home with a sitter.

Helen was punished in the best possible way — by feeling the natural and legitimate consequences of her own disobedience. She learned what could happen — and why — if she did not take care of her things as she had been taught. Her mother also avoided an open confrontation, which is *always* desirable. Nor did Helen get the satisfaction of "winning" by having her mother pick up after her, or by becoming the object of a "scene." From then on, while far from perfect, she improved greatly.

The next step beyond teaching your child to put away his own possessions and to keep his own room neat, is to teach him his responsibilities toward the rest of the house. You cannot, of course, expect a two-year-old to understand his responsibilities beyond his own domain. But, by the time he is between three and four, his sense of being a part of a family should make him ready to share in the care of community property. As I mentioned, what he does in his own room hurts only himself; the mess he leaves in the family rooms hurts everyone.

One intelligent young mother successfully broke her five-year-old Melinda of leaving her toys all over the house in this way. She told Melinda that she would not pick up Melinda's things for her in her own room, but, because she wanted the house neat when Daddy came home or guests were expected, she would pick up the toys in the living room if Melinda did not do so herself. She warned Melinda that she might not like the results. She then asked her husband to make a tall, narrow box that opened only at the top, with a cover with a stiff catch. This box was kept in the hall closet, and all the toys that Melinda did not put away were tossed into it. It was all Melinda could do to open the box and reach to the bottom of it, when she wanted a special toy. She soon found it easier to put her toys in her room, where she could easily get at them, than to struggle with the box. Again, the point was brought home, by the natural outcome of the action taken. Melinda learned a lesson, not only in neatness, but in cooperation and responsibility. And, since her mother had warned her what would happen if she refused to pick up her things, there was no disastrous confrontation.

Here is another way of coping with the problem of possessions scattered all over the house. Warn your child that you will have to pick up the things which are in your way if he will not do it, but do not tell him where you will put them. Make it quite clear that you are not picking up for his sake, but for your own. Since you have had to pick the things up, you have every right to put them wherever you wish, and no particular obligation to tell him where they are. When enough of his belongings disappear in this manner, your youngster may well decide he had better start to do his own picking up. When he does, you can return his possessions, as long as he agrees that he will continue to take care of them.

If you have managed to "hold the line" for some time and have not given in to the urge to put your youngster's room in order, it may well have become such an overpowering mess that the mere idea of cleaning it up is too discouraging to him. This is the time to step in and offer some help. If he agrees, don't do it *for* him — do it *with* him. There is nothing to be gained by stubbornly refusing to cooperate with him once he wants to try. Make a pleasant joint effort out of the job, and he may be so pleased with the contrast that he will ask for your help and approval sooner — before things get into such a state.

Promptness

Promptness — or lack of it — is a very revealing indication of one's degree of personal orderliness. A person who never arrives anywhere on time is generally sloppy in other ways, too. The one who keeps his appointments punctually, and is concerned about the inconvenience he causes by being late, usually cares about his appearance, and keeps his home and his affairs in order.

We all know people who are chronically late; about whom we say, "We'll ask them to come at seven but we'll plan for them at eight." At the other extreme are those who are compulsive time-keepers. They are always the first guests to arrive, and when traveling, get to the airport so early that they may catch the plane ahead of the one on which they were scheduled.

These traits often seem to be inherited, or at least absorbed, from one's parents. Children whose mother and father allow an hour for a trip which takes fifteen minutes tend to grow up with the same habit. Those whose parents have very little sense of time, do not seem to acquire it elsewhere. Therefore, it is especially important for you to set a good example in this area. When you start to raise a family, mend the bad habits which seemed unimportant before, and try to instill in your children a sensible and reasonable approach to being on time.

When your child is between four and five he is old enough to understand the plain inconsiderateness of being late. Explain that while it may not make any difference to *him* if he is ready and waiting for his car pool to pick him up for nursery school, it makes a great deal of difference to the other children and the driver. If his slowness causes the group to be late, the others, through no fault of their own, will be penalized as much as he will. In many cases, it is simply *not fair* to keep people waiting.

Don't let your child's habit of lateness disrupt the rest of your family. They — like the children in the car pool — should not be penalized or inconvenienced by his carelessness, laziness, or deliberate disobedience.

To be fair to your youngster, you must be sure that he knows exactly what is expected of him. It is impossible for him to be on time for dinner if you say, "Be home in time for dinner, Jake," without telling him that dinner will be ready at 6:30. When he is very young — preschool age — you must follow up such instructions by giving him a warning period. At 6:15 try to find him — whether he is playing in his room, out in the yard, or at your next-door neighbor's — and remind him that dinner will be ready in fifteen minutes. This is essential, of course, when he is too young to tell time, but when he is that young he will undoubtedly be with you or very close by. Many parents whose youngsters are old enough to run about the neighborhood by themselves use a cowbell or a whistle to call them in. As long as the children can recognize their own signal, this seems more dignified than screeching at the top of your lungs. The main thing is that you ring your bell or blow your whistle an agreed-upon fifteen or twenty minutes ahead of the hour the child is expected home. This allows him time to finish his game, say his good-byes, make his plans for tomorrow, and wash up for dinner.

If you cannot get your youngster to abide by your rules, don't make the mistake of giving in to his disobedience. Don't put his dinner on the hot plate and give it to him at whatever hour he arrives. Worse yet, don't make something else for him if his dinner is ruined by the delay. Tell him — and stick to it — that dinner will be served at 6:30, and *no one* will be served after that. If he is not there, he will go hungry because no "snacks" later will be allowed.

Unless your child is ill or terribly underweight, it will not hurt him to miss a few dinners, if that becomes necessary. Even your "growing boy" probably eats more than is necessary to maintain good health. So don't let your sympathy overcome your resolution to teach him promptness. For several days — or more — he may think he is surviving happily on two meals a day with some afternoon snacks to tide him over.

Sooner or later, however, he will start to miss his evening meal, as well as the company of the rest of the family. When he does, don't make too much of an issue of it. Let him know you are glad he is back at the dinner table, and give him one or two of his favorite dishes. He will soon realize that the half hour of extra play he gained when he was late was not worth a good meal and his parents' approval.

The "Reverse" Example

If you are truly desperate — if your best efforts, your reminders, your lectures, and your punishments have failed to instill a sense of orderliness in your youngster — there is one more remedy before you give up or resort to open warfare. Neither of which accomplishes anything but disaster. It requires considerable effort and resolution on your part, so reserve it for a "last stand," but it *is* effective. It is the "If you can do it, so can I" routine. Dr. Rudolf Driekurs, in his book *Children, the Challenge*, gives an excellent example.

Four-year-old Doris was making no progress at all in learning to pick up after herself, or care for her clothes or her toys. Her mother, in desperation, attended a Child Guidance Clinic, and was given an excellent suggestion. The next morning Doris made the usual mess about the house. Her mother asked her if she wouldn't like to put her toys away before lunch. When Doris said, "No," Mother said, "Would you like to have a whole day when you don't have to put anything away?"

"Of course!"

"All right," replied Mother, "but may I have the same kind of day?"

"Sure," said Doris.

All the rest of the day, Mother left everything just where it happened to be. She left Doris' laundered clothes, and her baby brother's diapers, all over Doris' bed. When she cooked lunch she left the dirty dishes and the baby's bottles and sterilizer on the kitchen table. When Daddy came home (he had been briefed about the plan) he dropped his coat on Doris' doll's carriage in the hall, threw his paper on the stairs, and settled down to read a magazine. Mother cooked dinner as usual, chatting pleasantly with Doris. When it was ready, she went and sat down with Daddy. Doris said, "I'm hungry."

Dad asked, "When will dinner be ready?"

Mother said, "It's ready but we can't eat."

"Why not?"

"Because there's no room on the table."

After a while, Doris began to grumble. "I'm hungry, Mom. I want my dinner, please."

Her mother smiled and shrugged her shoulders, and went on reading.

After a bit more grumbling, Doris disappeared into the kitchen. When she came back she said, "I've cleaned the table. Can we have dinner, now?"

Mother set the table and they had a pleasant dinner with no recriminations or "morals" being pointed out.

Later, when Doris was ready to go to sleep, she found her bed covered with fresh laundry and piles of diapers. "I don't like this, Mom," she said, and burst into tears.

"Well, what shall we do?" asked her mother.

"Let's pick it up so I can get into bed." With her mother's help, Doris cleared her bed and put away her clothes.

Because Doris' mother avoided a confrontation, kept the atmosphere friendly, and made the situation perfectly natural, it was a success. She could not do this often, but for some time a mere reminder of "the day we didn't pick up" was enough to keep Doris from falling back into her old ways.

This same method exactly may be applied to personal appearance and to promptness.

Children like to feel proud of their parents, and at

quite a young age are conscious of how Mom and Dad look — especially when they are "dressed up." While, under normal circumstances, parents should try at all times to set a good example as far as good grooming and neatness go, a little reverse psychology can be effective here, too.

I know of one mother who cured her daughter, Julie, of wearing too-heavy makeup by meeting her at school one day (where the girl's friends would surely see her) with an even heavier coat of paint. Her false eyelashes kept slipping, giving her a unique squint. The heavy application of purple lipstick changed the shape and expression of her mouth. Her hair was wrapped in a zebra-striped turban. Julie walked right past the car, saying, "I wonder who has a car exactly like ours." Her friend Joan looked back, and did a double take. "Julie, that's your mother!" she exclaimed, in horror. Later Julie and her mother had a good laugh about it, but Julie got the point.

If your problem is in the area of promptness, you may very easily put your point across with the "I can do it, too" approach. Start out in the morning by serving breakfast so late that your youngster almost — not quite — misses his ride to school. Then, when you pick him up after school, arrive ten or fifteen minutes late. Let him know how it feels to be kept waiting. If you are taking him to play with a friend or to an after-school activity, get him there fifteen or twenty minutes late — enough to embarrass him. When he complains, point out that if he won't make the effort to be on time when you ask him to, neither should you be required to be on time because it would be convenient for him.

In short, if you can *demonstrate,* by your own actions, the error of his ways, without anger, or nagging or criticism, you will have taken a giant step forward. The lessons, particularly for very young children, must be simple and obvious. But that kind of example — visual, or concrete in some other way — is worth a million words, especially words that are angry, unrealistic, or repetitive.

Table Manners

From High Chair to Table

When mothers ask, "At what age should I start to teach my baby table manners?" I answer, "From the very beginning." This may sound exaggerated but it is possible, and the best way. The very first lesson your baby can absorb is that of neat, clean eating. If, when you start giving him cereal or fruit from a spoon at the age of two or three months, you clean up his dribbles, burps, and spits each time they occur, and you keep him clean and comfortable throughout his feeding periods, he will learn to like it that way. It will be many months before he will do it himself, but those months will be easier for you if he welcomes cleanly habits and does not fight your efforts to wipe his mouth, wash off his hands, and so on.

The real "teaching" of table manners starts when your child first indicates a desire to try eating by himself. This varies tremendously — some babies want to hold their own spoon or cup almost as soon as they can sit in a high chair. Others are lazier, or enjoy the attention and care they get when their mothers feed them. Don't force him before he is ready — your troubles will multiply once he starts! During those months before your baby starts to feed himself, his learning will be mostly confined to observation — to watching when *you* eat. Even though his meal hours are different from yours, it is a great help to let him sit in his high chair with you while you and your husband eat. Give him bread or a cookie to chew on, talk to him, give an occasional taste of your food. He will soon learn that mealtime is an enjoyable occasion. And young as he may be, he will be watching you and storing up in his mind a picture of your manners which will then come to him more easily when he starts to feed himself.

The necessary equipment to help your child help himself consists of a baby spoon, a hot-water warming plate, a solid, unbreakable mug, and a good, big bib. If you have not been given a silver baby spoon, try a plastic picnic spoon, which is very light, and like the baby spoon, has a short handle. It is the handle which is important. The baby has far more control over a spoon which he can grip near the bowl than one with a long, thin shaft. The hot-water plate will keep his food tastier and more appetizing even though he dawdles, and therefore he will be more amenable toward finishing what is served him. Plastic or disposable bibs are a joy — they are more for your benefit, obviously, than the baby's. Your patience and good nature will be greatly enhanced if you know that the inevitable slops and drips don't mean extra laundry or ruined clothes. Get the big cover-up kind when your baby starts to feed himself — a mere wipe with a sponge or an occasional rinse in soapy water will keep your child looking cute and clean, and your disposition to match.

In the beginning, it doesn't matter at all *how* your child holds his spoon. Any way that will get the food from plate to mouth is acceptable. You may have to show him which way is "up" at first, but otherwise let him hold it as he wishes, including whether he chooses his right or left hand. Shortly, you may encourage him occasionally to eat with his right hand by handing him the spoon on that side, but if he switches it to the left, let him alone.

Even though he may still have a bottle, or be nursing when he is several months old, give him some of his milk or other liquid in a small plastic mug or tumbler. The tumbler is actually safer because there is no temptation to try to pick it up by a handle — a precarious effort for a baby. The tumbler should be lightweight, but the baby should be taught to pick it up with two hands. He will progress from that to using a mug with a handle in one hand, and when his hands are large enough to use one only, a regular "orange juice" or other small glass.

It is perfectly natural for babies to spit, blow, and "Bronx cheer" their food. It will require a good deal of patience on your part to get through this stage without a crisis, but try. If you make an issue of it each time your youngster blows, the habit will get much more deeply imbedded. He will enjoy not only the noise and the fun of spitting, but he will enjoy the attention and excitement he is generating with you. He will also undoubtedly find that he can get extra attention by throwing his food or spoon on the floor, or upsetting his plate or mug. Again, the key word is patience. As long as you are sure that he is physically capable of managing his utensils, start telling him that he is naughty, and that's not the way things are done. Clean up his mess as calmly as you can, and encourage him to eat some more. In the case of throwing his food or implements on the floor, pick them up for him once or twice — it *could* be a mistake, after all — and then tell him you will not do it again. If he repeats the action, simply take him from the high chair and put him down for his nap, into his playpen, or whatever is scheduled. Whatever you do, don't give him another helping. It will not hurt him to miss a part of one or two or three meals, and he will soon learn that such naughtiness backfires. He will receive less attention rather than more because mealtime will end faster, and there will be no exciting battle for him to look forward to.

Through all his experiments and efforts, try *not* to criticize or nag continually. Of course you must correct him, but do let him experiment and practice and have a little *fun* out of his meals. Encouragement and praise will pay off. Children *like* to live up to your expectations, and if you let them know what you want, and show how pleased you are when they succeed, your enthusiasm will win their cooperation as no amount of punishment could ever do.

There is also a great temptation to laugh at a baby who has smeared chocolate pudding all over his face. Don't do it and don't let older children do it. If it was an honest mistake or lack of skill, you will hurt his feelings and discourage him from trying to feed himself. If he did it on purpose to gain attention, you will be playing right into his hands and encouraging him to do it again. Let him know you don't think he has done well, clean him up, and ask him if he would like to try again to do better.

A mother who has a finicky eater may resort to all sorts of diversions in order to get her baby to eat. I would like to say a word about not using toys for this purpose. If a child learns that it is acceptable to play with anything at the table, he will transfer that pattern to playing with his silver or other items when he moves on to the family table. Also, the habit of actually taking games or toys to the table may become difficult to break. You may think up any games, stories, or any imaginative distractions you can to break down his resistance and take his mind off the fact that he is eating, but make them intangible distractions rather than "solid" ones.

Your baby will probably graduate to using a knife

and fork as well as a spoon while his hands are still too small to grasp the implements in the accepted adult way. If he has a baby knife and fork, you can start to teach him the correct way of holding those, but if he moves from a baby spoon directly to a large fork, you will have to wait until he is perhaps two and a half to three years old.

When he starts using a fork, he should hold it tines up, with his fingers in much the position used for holding a pencil. It will be awkward for him at first, but with patient instruction from you, he will soon become accustomed to the position. He should be shown the use of a "pusher" at this time — using a small piece of bread, or the edge of his knife to guide food onto his fork.

When he is ready to try using a knife, start him with easy meats, such as a piece of liver, a slice of chicken breast, or a thin piece of veal. These are tender and boneless and will not discourage him. To cut, he holds the knife with his right hand on top of the handle, index finger pointed down toward the blade to apply pressure. He holds the fork in the same manner in his left hand, with the tines down to hold the meat. Then, you may teach him either of two ways. When he has cut off the desired mouthful, he may put it directly into his mouth with the fork still held in his left hand, tines down. This is the "European" method. Or he may put the knife down, turn the fork tines up, and transfer it to his right hand to put it into his mouth. This is the "American" method. Either is perfectly correct, but because the American "zigzag" way seems unnecessarily complicated to me, I recommend the European style of eating.

At this stage your child should be shown how to cut soft foods with the side of the fork and the use of the butter knife. A slice of bread should be broken into two or three pieces and buttered on the butter plate, or if there is no butter plate, on the edge of the dinner plate — not on the palm of the hand. Rolls, too, should be broken into two or three pieces.

When he is four or five, and old enough to have his meals with you, his instruction in general behavior at the table must start in earnest. In order to get him interested in learning about table manners, he must be convinced that they are worthwhile. There are a number of good arguments available to help you convince him. First, stress the fact that dinnertime is the hour of the day that grown-ups look forward to most. Therefore, it should be as pleasant as possible. Anyone old enough to join in is expected to add to that pleasure — not to be a disturbing influence. Give him a choice — ask him if he thinks he is ready to do that. Emphasize that *you* think he is, and he will be making you very happy by showing that he is old enough and capable enough to join the family. You can then, one at a time as the problems arise, point out to him why certain manners "work." Show him how unattractive you look chewing with your mouth open, or what happens (even at the expense of a wasted mug of cocoa) if he leaves the spoon in his cup.

From there on, as he gets old enough to go out to dinner with you occasionally, you can continue to appeal to his own pride, and you can introduce the matter of family pride.

If you follow this line consistently, your child will accept the methods you teach him with very little question and eventually will realize that good manners do make eating more fun and easier for everyone, as well as making him and the others present more attractive to each other.

He must begin by learning:

Not to reach across people for anything, but to ask the one nearest the item he wants to pass it.

To put jelly or condiments on the butter plate or edge of the dinner plate rather than directly onto bread or meat.

To ask to be excused if he wishes to leave the table before everyone is through.

To place spoons on a plate or saucer — never to leave them in a cup or glass.

To swallow a mouthful of food before taking a drink.

To keep his plate "neat" — not messing everything into one big hash.

Not to shove his plate away when he is through.

Not to squiggle, squirm, or lean on the table.

Not to play with implements or the napkin, or draw on the tablecloth or mat.

Not to overload his fork.

And finally — the two most important rules.

To eat silently — he must not slurp, or chew audibly (mouth open). If he has to cough or sneeze, he covers it up with his napkin.

To eat "invisibly" — he must always chew with his mouth closed. He must learn to wait until his mouth is empty to talk — even in reply to a question.

Teaching your youngster basic table manners requires a great deal of time and patience. While he is a baby, try to arrange his meal hours so that you can devote that time to him without distractions. Feed him before your husband comes home. Your attention will not be divided, and the baby will be contented and ready to spend a play period with his dad. Meal-time should be different from playtime, but it should also be fun. Try to make it pleasant for your baby, and try to enjoy it yourself. If you look forward to it, and regard it as a time when you will enjoy each other's company, so will your baby. When you hear a mother say, "I know her manners are terrible, but she's just a baby," you are really hearing an excuse. She simply is not willing or able to devote the time to her child during meal hours that she should and could. If you want to do it badly enough you can find time, and I urge you to do so. It will pay off a thousand times over, in your pleasure and pride in your child, and his joy in eating and pride in his own accomplishments.

Surroundings and Atmosphere

The surroundings your youngster encounters at mealtime have a tremendous influence on his manners. An effort on your part to make the table attractive with pretty mats (disposable paper ones are ideal for everyday), a little ornament in the center, and nicely set places will more than be repaid by your family's enthusiasm. Even more important is the atmosphere you create. Digestion and appetite are both upset by bickering, unpleasantness, and even by boredom. Try to stimulate every member of the family — including the youngest — to contribute to general conversation. Don't allow your children to start arguments. At the first unpleasant remark Billy makes to his sister, "You haven't paid me back the quarter you owe me," for example, say quietly, "Billy, that subject can wait until we leave the table. How was football practice today?" The dinner hour is generally the only time of the day that the family is all together, and it should be an event to look forward to. Insist that all your family eat at the same time, and include your baby in the hour just as soon as he is old enough to enjoy it. Even, as mentioned earlier, before he actually eats with the older members. There is no other opportunity so ideal for strengthening family ties and stimulating interest and enthusiasm for each other and for projects and plans.

It is not always easy to establish a delightful atmosphere at the table, especially if you have not tried to make mealtime fun from the day your baby first sat in a high chair. And sometimes parents, tired and irritable after a difficult day, use the dinner hour as a time to work off their frustrations by picking on their children for the slightest slips. This is something husband and wife should discuss. You must *never* contradict each other in front of the children, so, in advance, try to agree on what you are trying to achieve and make up your minds to cooperate. If all else fails, one can fall back on the reverse twist as a shock treatment.

A mother named Mrs. Perry found an interesting way to improve the atmosphere at her dinner table. The children grumbled about everything — being on time, washing their hands, and the choice of menus. They took the serving of the meal as a signal to relate all their grievances — complete with accusations, arguments, and insults. Mrs. Perry, in desperation, said, one night, "Since everyone dislikes dinnertime so much and it is so unpleasant, why don't we give it up? You can all eat in your own rooms. How would you like that?" The three children, ages three to ten, thought it would be fine. "All right," said Mrs. Perry, "you carry your own trays to your rooms, and you bring them back to the kitchen. If you do that, I will wash the dishes." Mr. and Mrs. Perry took their own trays to the dining room, and ignored the children. After a week had passed, half the dinner plates were still in the rooms and even the children were tired of looking at the dreary leftovers. Mrs. Perry steadfastly refused to go for the dishes. The children began to complain. They found that eating by themselves was boring. Mr. Perry suggested a family meeting. Everyone was asked how he felt about the new system; the vote was unanimous. The children all wanted to come back to the dining room. Mr. and Mrs. Perry said "fine," on the condition that there would be no more complaints or arguments. The children readily agreed, and afterwards only needed to be reminded of "The Week of Trays" to stop any arguing before it started.

Developing Tastes

Eating can be the greatest fun in the world. Or it can be deadly dull. To me it seems very sad, as well as very rude, to have a child say, "Ugh, I hate that," or "What's that awful-looking stuff?" It's also a strong indication that that child has never been urged to try anything new, or has always been fed just the things he thinks he likes best. Mothers are tempted to do just that because they know the youngster will probably finish his meal without a fuss, but they are doing him a great disservice. I do not suggest that a child be given a new dish and forced to eat it all, whether he likes it or not. That is a sure way of turning him against *anything* unfamiliar. I do suggest that you urge your child to take one or two tastes of new dishes regularly and frequently. Start out with things that you are *sure* he will like until he becomes accustomed to the idea that a new dish is something to look forward to. Then, occasionally slip in a trial taste of something less sure-fire. If he doesn't have a built-in resistance to anything strange, he may surprise you with his reaction. I certainly almost fell over when my eight-year-old son swallowed his first little neck clam, smacked his lips, and asked for another! Dishes which he does not *dis*-like should then be served to him in very small portions occasionally until they *are* familiar to him. How many men do you know who shy away when their wives try to prepare anything other than the ubiquitous steak, chops, roasts, or chicken? There is nothing wrong with any of these, of course — in fact they can all be superb — but there are so many other equally fine dishes that these men — and their children — miss, because they have never been exposed to them. It's too late, perhaps, to change your husband's tastes, but it is just the right time to start your child toward an appreciation of more varied menus and exciting foods.

Again, try to get your husband's cooperation. Even

if he is not impressed with one of your efforts, ask him not to make remarks about it. The children may not notice if he leaves most of it on his plate, but they can't fail to catch on to his feelings if he says, "That meat is practically raw," or "This chicken is all dried out," and so on. The youngsters at the table will quickly follow his lead, and that will be one more dish on the "no good" list. Furthermore, with his example to follow, they will soon start to criticize the food themselves. On the other hand, you and your husband can encourage them to expand their tastes by praising the food when it is especially good.

Aside from the fact that "ugh" demonstrates an unfortunate lack of open-mindedness in experimenting with food, it is rude. It should be discouraged on both scores. A friend of mine has hit upon an effective way of discouraging her seven-year-old boy from "ughs," gagging noises, and other graphic forms of protest. Whenever he lets his feelings be known this way, she starts screwing up her face, eye-wiping away the crocodile tears, and letting out a few sobs and wails. Her son (and his older sister, too) think their mother is a riot and she keeps the atmosphere happy. After they've had their laugh, she talks to him seriously, pointing out that she worked hard to prepare the dish, and even though he doesn't like it, he's being mean to her when he indicates it's *that* bad. She admits she doesn't expect him to like everything — any more than she does. And she stresses the fact that a simple "No more, thanks" would show his dislike without hurting her feelings. For this method to be successful, your child must have already learned the importance of consideration, and if you have put that lesson across, this one works.

Once your child is out of his high chair, and actually eating with you at the table, he should be expected to conform to your rules. And rules you should have, because this is where your youngster first encounters the necessity of good social behavior. It is up to you to set the standards and the values by which you expect your household to run, and to see that they are observed.

Your meals should be served at a designated hour, and your youngsters should be ready to answer your call, "Dinner's ready," promptly. The "warning system" was discussed earlier in this chapter, pages 153 to 155. They should also remain at the table until everyone is through — within reason. If you and your husband decide to linger over a cup of coffee, or if one of the children is dawdling, it is only reasonable that the other youngsters may leave the table. They must never do so, however, without asking if they may be excused. There are other legitimate reasons for leaving the table early although these apply mostly as the children get older — a friend coming by to pick them up, a movie starting-time, or a load of homework. The telephone is not an excuse for leaving the table. If a child answers when it rings during dinner, and the call is for him, he should learn to say, "I'm at dinner — I'll call you back as soon as we are through." If it is for someone else, he takes down the name and number, and explains that his sister will call back. You and your husband, in order to set a good example, should follow the same rule.

Letting very small children help set the table and having older children help with the serving and clearing away is excellent training. *All* children should help share the daily "drudgery" chores, and an equitable division of labor should be discussed and agreed upon by the entire family. Duties should be rotated — Sally sets table one week, washes one week, and dries the next, while Bobby follows the same schedule one week behind. You can work out your own system, but I do not believe that Mother should be stuck with all the dirty work, nor that boys should be allowed to get out of it because cooking and cleaning up were once considered a woman's domain. Daily chores are *family* responsibilities — not man's or woman's, and the boys who learn this early will have much happier marriages of their own.

The Left-Handed Child

If your child, when he is small, is ambidextrous, as many children are, you will be doing him a favor by teaching him to eat right-handed. In the future when he sits at a crowded table, he will find it very inconvenient to be eating with his left hand while his neighbors are eating with their right hands. He cannot avoid some elbow-bumping and jostling. It will also be easier for him if he learns to use a serving spoon with his right hand. Food is passed on the left, and it is extremely difficult and awkward to get one's left hand up to help oneself if the dish being served is held close, as it must be in close quarters.

For many years, the left-handedness was considered a great problem. Parents tried to force children to be right-handed. The next stage was to allow a child to use whichever hand seemed easier. I have consulted eminent pediatricians and the consensus is that a mother can easily tell if a child has a predilection or strong tendency to use one hand or the other by the time he is a year old. If, at that age, he usually reaches for objects with his left hand he should not be pressured into using his right hand. If he reaches with either hand, it cannot harm him to encourage him to use his right hand.

If you think about it, however, the manner in which the places are set in many ways favors the left-handed eater. The butter plate is on the left. The fork — your most-used implement — is on the left, and the salad plate, if one is used, is on the left side. It is surely no more problem for a left-handed child to reach across to pick up his glass or his spoon on the right than it is for the right-handed child to butter his bread on the left.

Never reverse the place-setting to favor his left-handedness. I repeat, it is no more difficult an arrangement for your left-hander than for your right-hander. The important thing is that you teach him to use the implements properly, in whichever hand he holds them. He must learn to adapt his habits to the normal setting, because that is what he is going to be faced with all his life. There is no reason why he cannot do it as easily as any other child, as long as you do not start him out wrong in a mistaken effort to make him more comfortable.

Bedtime

In many otherwise smooth-running households, the children's bedtime is often a battlefield. To avoid this, or to prevent it before it starts, takes a good deal of patience and imagination.

No normal child looks forward to the moment when he is told he must stop what he is doing, leave the company of the rest of the family, and go to bed. But with a little ingenuity, bedtime can become an occasion he accepts — even looks forward to — rather than dreads.

Some diversion — something to take the child's mind off the fact that he is being left alone — is effective. Even a small baby objects less to being put down in his crib if he has a mobile to watch or a music box or records to listen to.

A little extra attention from you and your husband at the bedtime hour will pay off. A continued story is an excellent device to make him look forward to that hour. When your imagination begins to run dry, you can repeat episodes, because young children love repetition — to hear over and over again a story or a poem they know. If you are not clever about make-believe, reading to your youngster is almost as effective. Again, you do not need a new story every night while he is small — he will happily listen to the same one time and again, and delight in being able to tell *you* what is going to happen.

If your child enjoys his bath, this is an ideal time to give it to him. Not only for the obvious sanitary reasons but because a warm bath is relaxing, and because it means that you and he will have fifteen or twenty minutes of fun together while he is being bathed.

In spite of every effort, four-year-old Bobby may still become one of the many youngsters who won't be distracted, and as he gets a little older, he simply refuses to go to bed when he is told. You can plead, threaten, punish, or bribe, but every night seven o'clock brings on a scene. You may, understandably, resort to force and drag him to bed, leaving him sobbing in his pillow. You may, equally understandably, give in to his pleadings and say, "Oh, all right, then — just fifteen minutes more." While understandable, neither outcome is desirable. The first results in increasing conflict between you and Bobby, and a rapidly developing hatred of going to bed on his part.

He will soon look at what should be a pleasant, normal function as something to be dreaded — even a form of punishment.

Giving in to a child may not be harmful to his attitude about bed, but it is disastrous to your relationship with him. He has "won" the contest of wills, and your authority is opened to question. If he can force you to give in to him by a little stubbornness and a show of temper in this instance, he will pursue the same course in other circumstances. It will become increasingly hard to hold the line.

The ideal solution is to avoid an open battle. Just as he enjoys your rage when he deliberately tips over his cereal bowl, so will he enjoy your rage at his refusal to go quietly to bed. Mad as you may feel, don't show it. Tell your child that his bedtime is seven o'clock, and that you will help him get ready for bed, you will read to him, and you will say good-night at seven-thirty. After that you will assume that he is going to sleep and pay no more attention to him. As in all other situations involving times, give him a warning call, so that he may finish what he is doing, and be mentally prepared for the final call.

Let us say that at 6:45 and again at 7:00 you tell Bobby that his bath is waiting and you are ready to help him. He is in the middle of a picture book so he says, "Not yet." A few minutes later you remind him you are waiting, and again he procrastinates. At seven-thirty he has still refused to budge and you say, "Good-night, Bobby." A short time later he comes to you and says, "I'm ready for my bath now."

"I'm sorry, Bobby, bathtime has passed. Good-night." This is the moment of truth. Having said "Good-night," you must stick to that line. No help with getting undressed, no reading, no tucking in. You *must* remain composed and aloof, no matter what tactics Bobby may use to provoke you. Although he may lose a few minutes' sleep each night for a time, his desire to make an issue out of bedtime will be thwarted. By ignoring his pleas, threats, tantrums, or whatever, you leave him with no target. He cannot carry on a battle if there is no opposition.

This, it is true, will not work with all children. There are some very strong, very active youngsters who will not give in to sleepiness, and very possibly will not give in to you, either. If, Bobby decides he would rather forego his bath and his storytime, and stay up as late as he chooses, you will have to take more direct action to insure that he gets enough sleep. The only answer is to take him to his room quietly but firmly, undress him, and put him bodily into his bed. Don't argue, don't scold, and pay no attention to his protestations. Say "Good-night" and leave, and make your-self unavailable — in your own room with the door closed if necessary. You must have your husband's co-operation, of course, or this type of discipline is useless. Again, the important thing is to avoid open warfare. By removing yourself from the scene, you leave Bobby with no adversary and he will soon get tired of throw-ing a tantrum for no one's benefit but his own.

A child should never be sent to bed as a punish-ment. That form of discipline cannot help but develop an unhappy reaction to going to bed at other times — especially when a youngster must stay in bed because he is ill. In addition to the fact that he is feeling miser-able, the sick child who has been punished in that way before may conclude that he has been "bad" — that his enforced stay in bed is a punishment. One little boy became terribly upset when his daddy was con-fined to his bed with flu. He was convinced that Daddy was being punished, and he was far more concerned about the fact that his much-admired father had done something wrong than that he was ill. Only the family doctor was able to convince him that the stay in bed was not a punishment, and the doctor also pointed out to the boy's mother the harm she was doing by using her child's bed as a means of discipline.

6

Conversation

Talk and Baby Talk

Learning to talk, as mentioned in Chapter 2, is surely the most demanding intellectual challenge a child faces. The result forms the basis for much of our behavior, and, at least outwardly, our intelligence. The child who speaks naturally, fluently, and correctly inevitably appears smarter — and more attractive — than the stumbling mumbler. Your speech, along with your appearance, creates society's impression of you.

When your baby is very tiny and responds only to tone rather than words, you will quite naturally talk to him in some form of baby talk. Every mother has her own special way of conversing with her baby, whether it is crooning, singsong, high- or low-pitched, or whatever. The baby quickly recognizes and responds to her "noises," and will also respond more readily to others who speak to him in the same way. This is fine for the first few months — the danger is that it may continue for too long. The first efforts your child makes to communicate with you will be in imitation of the sounds you make to him. If you laugh, he will try to laugh, if you squeal, his response will be his interpretation of a squeal, and so on. Therefore, as soon as he does begin to "talk" to you, you must start speaking to him in a normal tone of voice — one that you would use to anyone else, and one that you would want him to copy.

Your child will learn to talk partly by imitation. As he starts to form words, it is vitally important that you use simple but normal language with him. If you say "wittle" instead of "little," or "num-nums" instead of "dinner" or "food," he will, of course, say it too. Would you *want* him to learn to speak in that way, only to have to un-learn it as he gets older? Of course not. So don't *teach* him baby talk — speak to him in simple words which he can understand, but words that he will use the rest of his life.

People who habitually talk baby talk to children clearly indicate that they think the youngsters are not intelligent — that they are inferior to adults. They use a tone, as well as words, that they would never use with a contemporary. Children are sensitive to this, and I have seen my own youngsters' reactions to some of my friends who talked "down" to them in that way. Even today, as adults, they have never been able to completely forget their early reactions and dislike.

Every mother should make an effort to listen to herself when she speaks to her child. Are you using false excitement or enthusiasm to catch his attention? Is there scorn or impatience in your tone? Are you yelling, to stress an order or a reprimand? Are you using the *same* tones you would in speaking to your husband, or a friend? If not, take stock of yourself. There are times when, to make your point or to exert necessary authority, you must use an exaggerated tone of voice. But it should only be done for a good reason. In every other circumstance a quiet, relaxed tone will be most effective with your child because it will not arouse antagonism, and it will induce him to speak in the same way.

Above all, beware of allowing yourself to scream at your child. You cannot possibly gain anything by it — all the shouting in the world will never result in obedience or cooperation. It can only create open conflict and this should be avoided at all costs. Furthermore, the child who is yelled at yells back, or retires into a shell, and there is nothing desirable about either reaction.

Your youngster's grammar and his pronunciation and his accent will inevitably be similar to yours. If you live in a region where there is a strong accent — the South or northern New England, for example — he will grow up with that accent. That is as it should be and adds flavor and interest to his speech. Even if your own grammar is poor, however, you should make every effort to correct his — provided you recognize his mistakes. If he is picking up bad habits from his friends, it is worthwhile to correct him until he naturally uses the proper word or phrase. An unusual accent is interesting — incorrect grammar or pronunciation is not. It will, as he gets older, merely sound uneducated.

To avoid nagging at your youngster's efforts, try to vary your means of correction. Don't, every time you must correct him, simply say, "That's wrong, say it this way." Make up some games. Pretend that you do not hear him until he corrects himself. Make believe that you do not understand, and give him a ridiculous answer when he uses a word or phrase incorrectly. Or, repeat his sentence, and ask him if he can spot his error and correct it. Make him *think* about what he is saying and how he is saying it, rather than teaching him only by rote.

The Art of Conversation

For the first few years of your child's life your efforts will be devoted simply to teaching him to talk. He will be learning new words and new phrases every day. At times he may seem to go backwards. He will suddenly stop using a word he has been enchanted with for weeks. But in due course he will put words together, he will ask questions and make sentences, and he will be truly able to communicate with you. At this point he must begin to learn that there are things one does not do in talking, just as there are objects he may not touch.

Children who have just learned to *really* talk are usually intrigued with the sound of their own voices. They are also accustomed to your encouragement and the attention you have been giving them and they find they can now use their new skill as a means of getting more attention. Many are real chatterboxes and that is fine, but they must be taught that there are some restrictions on their chatter.

Children should never be allowed to interrupt. This

is part of learning that they are members of society and must respect the rights of other people in that society. No matter how boring they feel the conversation is, or how important their contribution, they must be taught to wait until there is a "break" before they speak. I have a friend whose small children continually run in and out while we are visiting, calling "Mommy, this," or "Mommy, that," as soon as they are inside the door. She invariably breaks off our conversation with "What is it, dear?" and of course it is never anything important. The children simply know that all they have to do is interrupt in order to get her attention. Those children will have a very difficult time when they have to adjust to regulations in school, or even to a group of their friends. Their mother could correct the situation by telling them that this was an hour in which she wished to talk to her friend without interruptions. She could give them a choice of playing outside with their friends, or going upstairs to their room to play. But it should be made quite clear that no running in and out would be permitted nor would she respond to any interruptions. If she would stick to this course during a few visits, the children would soon turn to more interesting occupations when their mother was entertaining.

To make this more palatable to the youngsters, my

friend might suggest a fair exchange of favors. Although I do not generally approve of offering rewards for good behavior, which should be expected as a matter of course, a reward "in kind" is sometimes helpful. In this case the children's mother might say to them, "Fair is fair. You amuse yourselves and let me have two hours to myself to visit with Mrs. Post this afternoon, and tomorrow, I will give you two hours of my time, to do what you want." This type of approach has the added advantage of making youngsters look forward to visitors, rather than feeling resentful of the intrusion on their domain.

Children who constantly break into other people's conversation — even their contemporaries' — must learn early in life — before they reach school age — that this is inconsiderate, selfish, and rude. If allowed at first it becomes a hard habit to break. In this case, once again, the tit-for-tat method of education is very effective.

If all your warnings, scoldings, and discussions have failed, try interrupting everything your child starts to say for a few days. At first he will be surprised, then confused, and later he will undoubtedly become angry. "Mother, *stop* it. Let me finish!" At this point sit down with him and explain that his interruptions have made you feel the same way. Now that he sees what it is like to be on the other end, perhaps he will understand what you have been trying to tell him.

Youngsters must also learn that out-and-out contradiction is rude. It would be impossible to completely stop children from contradicting each other, but they can be taught that they must not contradict their elders. Nothing sounds cockier, ruder, and more disrespectful than a flat contradiction. Your child has every right to disagree with any statement, but teach him to say, "Are you sure you did?" or even "I didn't *think* you did," instead of "You did not!"

There is one very simple thing you can urge your child to do which will make him sound wonderfully polite and which will also help instill in him respect for older people. That is, teach him to add a name after his responses. How much friendlier "Yes, Mom" sounds in response to your call than just "Yes" or "Yeah." When your youngster meets your friends, he should say not just "Hello" or "How do you do?" but "Hello, Mrs. Smith." Mrs. Smith will love it, and if he has just met her, it will help him to remember her name.

"Bad" Language

No matter how careful you and your husband are about using "bad" language — either swear words or so-called four-letter words — in front of your child, he is going to hear them sooner or later, and he is going to try them out on you. When he is very little, he and his friends may well go through a stage when they think "toilet" words or words relating to the body are funny. They may go into fits of giggles over such words as "popo" or "wee-wee," or "fanny." This is perfectly normal, and if you make nothing of it, they will soon get over it. "Wee-wee" and "pee-pee" are universally used and understood, and there is really nothing objectionable in their use. As your child matures, he will naturally acquire more modesty in regard to bodily functions, and will probably, of his own accord, switch to "I want to go to the bathroom, Mommy." Unless you have a particular aversion to any of those words, don't react at all. If you do have a reason you would rather they didn't use the word, suggest another, rather than prohibiting the use of that one. Forbidding the use of a word is the surest way to make it attractive!

The question of "four-letter words" or sex terms is far more complicated today than it was a generation ago. Words considered absolutely unmentionable then are now commonplace, and used by refined, educated people. The language of the younger generation is liberally sprinkled with words which shock many older people to the core. Every novel that is printed and every play on Broadway is filled with language that would never have gotten past the censors a few short years back. And yet few parents, no matter how liberal, want to hear their four-year-old say, "Oh s——t!"

So what are you going to tell your child? First, when he comes home from school with a new word in that category, you should ask him if he knows what it means, and, if he doesn't, you should tell him. Then you can explain to him that there are people who are upset by words relating to sex or to bathroom functions and therefore, because you would rather he didn't go around offending people, you would prefer him to find another expression. One father told his nine-year-old, "Look, that word doesn't bother me particularly, but I know Mom doesn't like it, so let's not use it around the house, O.K.?" This puts the emphasis on the right spot — the word itself isn't so important, but the fact that it may offend, is. Let your child know which words may be objectionable, and to what audience, and suggest that he use other terms in specific situations. In school, he is surely going to use all the same language that his classmates use, and it will bother no one, but he should be taught which of those words he can bring home — or to his grandmother's!

A Show of Respect

Respect for his parents, and for all adults, is an integral part of a well-brought-up child. It is all very well to be "pals" with your child, but you are *not* the same age, nor can you have the same abilities or the same interests. There is little to be gained by pretending that you do. An attitude which accepts and takes advantage of the age difference, is far more satisfactory. You have lived longer, you have vastly more experience, and therefore you have a great deal to offer. Your child, in receiving and assimilating the fruits of your experience, will automatically develop a respect for you. But to keep that respect you must not only earn it, but foster it.

One simple mark of recognition of the difference in status is the use of a title for adults. If you deny your position as parents by rejecting the use of "Mother" or "Father" or their derivatives, you are inevitably undermining your natural parent-child relationship. You are trying to be a sister or brother rather than a mother or father. You are taking away from the child the comfort and strength that "Mother" and "Father" represent. He can find all the friendship he needs with his peers — he can only find the security he needs with real parents who accept the relationship and are proud of it.

In most cases, children should be taught to carry this respect on to other adults. Their mother's and father's friends are Mr. and Mrs. Brooks, and there is nothing old-fashioned or stuffy in using those titles. However, some adults — especially very young newly marrieds — prefer that their friends' children do use their first names. This is certainly their prerogative, and if they ask the children to call them Hank and Sue, the children should comply. But you, as a parent, should make it very clear to your child that this is a special case and he is only to use those names because it was requested.

In this day of part-time help — cleaning women, sitters, or dinner-party caterers — there is sometimes confusion about what the children should call the employee. In general, they should use the same form of address that you do. Older women who come in to "sit" are called "Mrs. Franklin" or "Miss Goldberg." Young girl sitters are called by their first names. Cleaning women are often called by their first names, but it is considerate to ask them what they would like you and the children to call them.

Your youngsters should never give orders to your household help. You are the employer, and you are the only one to do that. If your daughter would like a blouse ironed, she may ask Mrs. McDonald if she would have time to do it, but she may not *demand* that Mrs. McDonald do it. In most cases it is better that children ask their mother to make the request and then there is no question of disrespect. The days of Annie, the chambermaid, who said "Yes, Miss Hilary" or "No, Master Frank" are gone and household help should be treated by your children with the same respect and courtesy they would show any other adult.

Telephone Manners

Most small children get a tremendous kick out of answering the telephone. Unfortunately, many of their mothers neglect to teach them the friendliest and nicest way to do it. In far too many homes the phone is picked up and a squeaky voice says, "Who's this?" or "Who are you?" without so much as a "Hello" first. It may sound "cute" when the child is very young, but it may *not* when he is older, and the habit, once installed, is hard to break.

When your youngster first shows an inclination to run for the phone, have a little talk with him. Explain that, because the other person cannot see him as if they were talking in the same room, he must remember certain things.

1. He must try to sound pleasant, because the caller cannot see his smile. Suggest that he try to put his smile into his voice.

2. He must speak slowly and clearly, because it is harder to understand when one cannot watch the speaker's mouth and face.

3. He must not shout because it hurts the ear of the person holding the phone at the other end.

Buy two toy telephones and illustrate your points by holding conversations with him on the toy phones. He will love the game if you make up silly names, and funny or exciting reasons for calling. When he has learned the right way to answer the phone, let him pretend he is making the call. Tell him that when he is doing it all correctly, he may graduate to the real phone.

The simplest and most accepted way of answering the telephone in the United States is "Hello," and that is what your child should say when he picks up the receiver. Then, when the caller asks for the person he wishes to speak to, and that person is home, the young-ster should learn to say, "Just a minute, please." If you wish, you may teach him to say, "Who is this, please?" Some parents like to know who is calling before they answer; others feel that the caller may feel the child is merely being inquisitive. So that is up to you, and either response is correct.

Presumably a child of that age (three to six, let us say) would never be left at home alone, so there is no need to discuss with him at this point what he should say if he is alone in the house. If he has been left with a sitter, and the call is for you, he should say, "Mommy is out, but I'll call Jean, my sitter." Jean can then take a message, or decide whether or not information should be given out as to where you are and when you will return, according to the caller's identity.

Once he has earned the right to answer the phone, be sure that he follows through. There is nothing more frustrating than hearing a child say, "I'll call her," in response to your "May I speak to your mommy?" and then disappear. You can hear the phone drop, you can hear one call of "Mommy, it's for you," and then silence. You can't even hang up and call again, because the line will be busy. So be *sure* that he understands that he must persist until you answer him. In fact, as soon as he has had a little practice, you should insist that he go back to the phone if you are delayed for a moment and say, "Mommy will be right here."

Let us go back for a moment to the safe procedure for the older child who may be alone in the house at times. It is sad but true that the telephone is occasionally used by criminals, cranks, or perverts to ascertain whether a house is empty, or whether there are children alone at home. Therefore it is most important that you teach your child *not* to give out any information unless he knows the caller. Hearing the name is not enough — he must know who the person is, either personally, or because he knows *you* know him.

The child should *never* say, "She's not here. Who is this, please?" He *should* say, "Who is this, please?" first. Then, if the name is unfamiliar or the caller refuses to give a name, the youngster says, "She's busy just now (or perhaps, "She's just across the street); if you'll give me your number she will call you back." If your youngster can handle big words, the phrase "She's not available just now" is excellent. It is vague, makes no commitment, but implies that the one called is at home. These replies clearly hint that the child is not alone, or mother is close by, and also help to establish the legitimacy of the call. The caller who has nothing to hide will not hesitate to give his number.

A year or two after Jamie starts to answer the phone, he may want to try to make some calls himself. He must wait, of course, until his fingers are strong enough to dial, and until he can remember or read seven digits. Until that day, you will simply have to be his switchboard operator when he wants to call a friend. When he is able to place his own calls, he must remember the proper routine, just as he did in answering incoming calls. The one really important thing to teach him is to identify himself at once. As soon as he hears "Hello" at the other end, he should say, "This is Jamie Lowe."

Then he asks for his friend, saying either "Is Alec there?" or "May I speak to Alec, please?" If he recognizes his friend as he answers, of course he need only say, "Hi, Alec, this is Jamie."

If everyone, adult and child, identified himself on the phone at the first opportunity, most of the confusion and occasional irritation that telephone calls create could be avoided. The responsibility to give his name at once falls on the person placing the call and every mother should give that rule number-one priority.

The Joy of Conversation

Along with the mechanics of talking, you will be failing your child badly if you do not teach him the sheer pleasure of conversation. You will also be missing a wonderful experience yourself. Nothing is more stimulating and more intriguing to a parent than to discover how his child's mind works, and how it develops. In addition, later in life it will result in his becoming a far more popular person, as well as more successful in his profession. Everyone enjoys being with a good conversationalist and the individual who earns that reputation is always in demand, both socially and in the business world.

It is a rare mother who, when her baby is very small, does not encourage him to talk without even thinking about it. "Say 'Bye-bye'," "Say 'Daddy'," "Say it after Mommy," start when the child is less than a year old. The response is, to say the least, minimal, but it is evidence that mothers can hardly wait for their children to start to communicate. Why, then, do so many parents turn their children off when they do begin to talk? The phrases "Stop that noise," "Be quiet, I'm reading," or just plain "Shut up, Johnny," are far more common in some houses than "Tell us about it." The parents who do this are in fact stunting their child's mental growth, as well as missing a great deal of fun themselves.

When your youngster is just learning to talk fluently, in his third year or so, encourage him constantly. Question him and help him to talk about daily events and to describe the new things he sees and each new experience he undergoes. Insofar as he can picture (imagine) what you are talking about, do the same for him. Don't talk down to him as you do this. Use simple words, but "adult" words that he is capable of assimilating into his own vocabulary.

When he is a little older, continue this questioning

in regard to what he *thinks* about his experiences. Expressing one's opinions effortlessly is not easy — even for an adult — and the earlier you encourage your youngster to start, the more readily he will be able to do it.

A wide vocabulary adds greatly to one's conversational skill, and when it is developed early it can improve the breadth of your child's imagination. It can also surprise and amuse you. Children use words they have picked up unexpectedly, often in the most unusual sense. Expressions inadvertently used by youngsters frequently become part of a family's special "personal" vocabulary and afford considerable amusement.

My husband woke up from a nap one day to find our three-year-old daughter had just spit on his forehead. "Cindy," he shouted, "what are you doing? You spit on me." "Oh, Daddy," she replied, "I didn't spit on you. You had dirt on your face and so I just 'put a little one' there to clean it." For years no one in our family "spit" — we just "put a little one."

It is almost as important to teach your youngster to be a good listener as to be a good talker. No conversationalist is a success unless he also knows how to give his sincere, undivided attention to the other person. Encourage your child to talk, surely, but also encourage him to listen to you. He will absorb this, partly, by your example. If you look at him while he is talking, if your expression shows your interest in what he is saying, if you ask the pertinent question at the right moment and make appropriate comments, he will tend to react the same way. Don't hesitate to help him more specifically, though. In case he hasn't copied your response to him, point it out. "Look at me while I'm talking." "Let me finish before you interrupt." After you have told him something, asking him questions to see how much he has absorbed will encourage him to listen well.

Most of all, have fun talking to your youngster, and getting him to talk to you. If *you* have fun, he will too, and it will be equally rewarding to you both.

7

As Others
See Your Child

When Company Comes

Very often, a child who seems to be rude or lacking in manners is that way simply because he doesn't know what he should do. Billy's mother calls him into the living room with no warning, and says, "Billy, this is Mrs. Wheelock. Shake hands with her." Billy has had little, if any, instruction in shaking hands so he hides his hands behind his back, hangs his head, and glowers. Billy, to all intents and purposes, is being rude.

To guarantee that your child will not react that way when company comes, be sure that he knows what is expected of him in advance. Some practice sessions in simple manners — shaking hands for boys, curtsying for little girls, saying "hello" with a smile, are essential. It need not be a grim business. With a little imagination you can make a game of it. Children love make-believe, and you can pretend you are four and your child is the stranger — Mrs. Bump-de-Bump, or any silly name you can think of. Tell him what to say, and how to shake hands with a little bow, and then change sides and make him practice it. Do this from time to time as soon as he is old enough to be expected to greet people properly, and it will soon become quite natural to him.

Then, *warn* him when you are expecting company. Tell him that you will be calling him in to meet old Mrs. Frothingham, and you will be very proud of him if he shows her how nicely he can shake hands. With the warning and the knowledge he will have no cause for shyness or rebellion, and you truly *will* be proud of him. If you also let him know he need not stay but can return to his play after saying "hello," he will develop a far friendlier attitude toward your visitors.

If Billy *does* panic when the moment arrives, don't make an issue of it. Disciplining a child in front of a stranger is never wise, and will only result in his disliking your friend and dreading other meetings. After your guest leaves, talk to him about how and why his greeting went wrong. Don't discourage him by scolding but keep it light, because if he was willing to try at all, he is probably somewhat embarrassed by his failure already. So, just talk casually about why one always uses his right hand to shake hands, or whatever his error may have been. Then, go back to practicing, perhaps inventing a new approach. Wait until you feel he is more at ease with these amenities before you put him in the same situation again.

If you are too insistent or too critical in regard to his meeting people, you run the danger of running into "I won't!" If possible, ignore it and don't force more introductions on him until he has had time to forget his embarrassment. But if it is a meeting which cannot be avoided, such as Great-aunt Millie's first visit since Billy was born, try the "reverse" line with him. "All right, Billy. If you won't come in and say hello to Aunt Millie nicely, don't ask me to do anything for you. I can say 'I won't,' too." Of course, your example is as important in this area as in all others. When Billy sees you shake hands with your friends, greet people enthusiastically and politely, stand up for older ladies, and so on, he will want to do the same. It is not fair to ask him to observe manners that you do not practice yourself. To instill a *desire* in children to be polite, husbands and wives must be very careful to see that they maintain a high standard of "manners" themselves.

Fathers have a particular responsibility in this, because little boys seem to have more natural resistance to polite handshakes than do little girls. By demonstrating that he enjoys greeting people enthusiastically, Dad can instill the idea that it's fun. His line with his son is that it's baby stuff to glower or to giggle, and that big men get real pleasure out of a firm handshake and a warm "Hi, there."

Some people think that bowing and curtsying are outdated — or seem affected. I feel that both gestures have a great deal of charm when a child is small. I also believe that they add another small step in the building of respect for older people. Curtsying should be forgotten when a girl reaches school age — it does appear affected in older children. But for very little children, both bowing and curtsying provide a useful crutch. It gives the youngster something to *do* — a routine to follow, and that is far easier for a child than to stand and do nothing.

Developing a firm handshake and a grin, and learning to look a person in the eye are more important than either curtsying or bowing. This, again, is a matter of practice, and it is worth the effort. No one cares for the person who gives a limp, "fishy" handshake, or looks down at the floor while he is saying "hello." The child who has learned to shake hands firmly and look right at the other person with a smile not only makes a good impression, but is developing his own self-confidence and self-respect.

With His Contemporaries

Children — even very young ones — have certain responsibilities to their own playmates, too. One very concrete reason for teaching your child about sharing, taking turns, and so on, is that a knowledge of how to get along with other children will make his first experience with school and the "outside" world far easier. I taught in a nursery school at one time, and I could spot immediately those children who either had not had friends to play with, or whose parents had not taught them the basic principle — treat your friends as you would have your friends treat you. It literally took them weeks longer to adjust to the group.

While your youngster is very small — two or three, let us say — most of his social activities will take place when your friends bring their children over to play. They will be under constant supervision by you and the other mother. This is the time to instill the above principle, so that it becomes completely natural to them.

Like all training, it takes patience. It also takes

cooperation on your friend's part, and you and she should agree beforehand on the methods you want to try. There are mothers who constantly defend their own children and invariably take their "side." They are doing nothing but harm. When the children emerge from under their mothers' wings, they will have a rude awakening. Not only will they no longer have the crutch of their mothers' support to lean on, but the selfish and self-righteous attitude they inevitably develop will make them thoroughly unpopular. It is not fair to a child to back him up when he is wrong, or to tolerate it when he behaves badly. You are only going to make life more difficult for him in the end. I have heard my daughter-in-law say, "I like Candy, but her child is impossible — he does anything and everything he wants to do. I just don't want Casey to play with him and pick up his habits." Don't, by your tolerance of your child's antisocial habits, put him in the unfortunate position of Candy's child.

In teaching your child to share, you need not deprive him of his fun. Be sure that there are enough toys, games, or outdoor swings, slides, and so on, to give the children a choice. When, as they inevitably will, they both want to play with the same object, don't take it away from the one who has it. Do your best to persuade the interloper to play with something else for the moment. He must learn "first come, first served," and when he sees someone playing with a toy, it does not follow that he can go up and take it away.

The sequel is, of course, that the child who has had a reasonable time to play with the most desirable toy, eventually must be persuaded to share it. Again, don't just take it away and give it to his playmate. A child's attention span is short. Watch for the moment it wanders, and then step in. "It's Johnny's turn now, Billy, to play with the blocks. Come over here because I have something else for you to do." In short, if you create a diversion rather than a crisis, the idea of turning over a plaything to someone else, of taking turns with it, will be easier to accept.

The first responsibility of a host or hostess is to see that his guests have a good time. The child who has learned to do this when he is very young is going to be a popular host when he grows up. You, presumably, don't tell *your* guests what they are to do unless you know that it is something they enjoy. You ask them, after dinner, if they would *like* to play a game of bridge or a hand of gin, or perhaps they would prefer carpet bowls or bumper pool. Whatever it may be, it is the *choice* that counts. Follow that course when you entertain yourself, and make sure that your child follows it, too.

Whether there are two children playing together or eight — in a preschool group, perhaps — insist on their taking turns in every possible way. If you are pushing them on the swing, teach them to stand in line for their turns, so that each one gets his full share of fun. Don't let them shove and push, and discourage the habit by putting the "pusher" back at the end of the line. These habits, well ingrained, will stand them in good stead all their lives.

The Reluctant Hostess

There is another situation which arises occasionally. Your friend Sue is coming to spend the afternoon and bringing her five-year-old, Susie. What obligations does your four-year-old, Wendy, have? Must she give up playing with her friends to entertain a child she doesn't know?

The answer is to find a compromise between teaching Wendy the responsibilities of a hostess, and at the same time, not imposing on her freedom with a situation which is not of her own making. Of course it may work out beautifully. Wendy's friends may be off with their mothers, or sick in bed, and she may be delighted to have a ready-made playmate. But this doesn't always happen and Wendy may have been asked to play with her best friend or the neighborhood group may have been asked to play in Nancy Neighbor's wading pool.

You may, and should, insist that Wendy come in to greet Sue and Susie when they arrive. Wendy should then ask Susie to join her and her friends at the pool. Preferably, you should suggest this to Wendy ahead of time, and she should issue the invitation herself. If you have not done that, make the suggestion yourself. Don't do it as an order, "Wendy, take Susie with you to Mrs. Neighbor's," but as a suggestion: "Wendy, I'll bet Susie would love to see the wading pool — why don't you take her along?"

If Susie agrees, all is well, but Susie may *not* want to leave her mother to go off with a stranger. In that case Wendy's obligation is to go and get some toys or games for Susie to play with. After a few minutes of showing her the things, and perhaps playing with her for a little while, Wendy may be excused to rejoin her friends. She has made an effort to be hospitable, and since the visit was basically arranged for *your* pleasure, not hers, her obligations are fulfilled.

Wendy must be made to see and understand the

difference between that situation, and the occasion when her friends are asked over for *her* pleasure. In that case, she may never go off and leave them alone under any circumstances.

When Your Child Is the Visitor

Any number of mothers, including myself, have had the happy experience of hearing a friend say, "Peter was the nicest guest — how did you ever teach him such beautiful manners?" — or words to that effect. In my case, at least, my jaw must have dropped to my knees! For months I had been trying to instill some table manners in Peter with practically no evidence of success. Apparently it was not wasted effort. Peter, for whatever reasons, had been resisting my instruction at home, but it had "sunk in" and he actually was able to practice it when he wanted to. And sure enough, in due course, he decided that it wouldn't hurt to let his knowledge show at home, too.

When your youngster is old enough to be left by himself at another child's home to play, you will probably be very concerned, at first, about how he will act when you are not around. It depends, of course, on how well you have done as a teacher at home. When he is approaching the age when you feel you *can* leave him without having him feel "lost" and when you can trust him not to create chaos in his friend's home, you should start discussing certain "property rights" rules with him. Explain to him that he should not do things in other people's homes which he, and you, would not expect them to do in his (your) home.

A list of dos and don'ts with which your child should be acquainted follows. Check up on him, too. Call his friend's mother and ask her if he thanked her when he left and if he played nicely while he was there. By doing that you will know where he needs further instruction. By following up, you can make him a popular visitor, and ensure him of other invitations in the future.

A well-behaved young visitor:

Says "hello" to his friend's mother, Mrs. Neighbor, when he arrives.

Minds Mrs. Neighbor — without argument.

Goes along, in general, with whatever his friend suggests. (The "host" should, of course, ask Billy whether he would like to do this or that. But he may not, so persuade Billy to be the amenable one.)

Says "good-bye" and "thank you" to Mrs. Neighbor.

Does not take food from the refrigerator or the cupboards without permission.

Does not "snoop" in drawers or closets.

Does not bother or interrupt Mrs. Neighbor.

Treats his friend's playthings and Mrs. Neighbor's furnishings with respect and reasonable care.

To show your youngster what you mean by your various suggestions, try this. After he has had a friend over, discuss — very casually — the friend's behavior. It must be done with great tact because any criticism will get your child's "back up" and he won't listen to you at all. You can get the message across very lightly and painlessly with a well-chosen remark or two. "That Jackie's a good guy, isn't he? Did you notice how he helped me pick up my tools when I finished fixing the radio?" Or, on the other hand, "Wow, Jimmie may be a funny guy, but he certainly is rough on the furniture. Maybe you'd better wait to have him over again until you can play outside." Then when your son is invited out himself, a reminder is in order. "Try to behave, won't you? Remember how we felt about Jimmie last winter?"

Children's Parties

Birthday parties are a very important event in a child's life and they provide his first experiences with social activities. They also provide his parents with the first opportunity to start teaching him the responsibilities of being a host or a guest. Organized social functions have been a mark of civilized people throughout the ages, and knowing how to participate in them is essential. It is all part of getting along with other people well, and showing consideration in one's relationships. The host who puts his guests' pleasure above all else, and the guest who shows his appreciation of his host's efforts, are generally *nice* people.

When your child's birthday rolls around, take advantage of the occasion to instruct, as well as to give him a good time. Discuss with him the fact that a host does have obligations as well as rights. He may be too young to absorb a great deal of this philosophical approach, but he can understand the simpler aspects, such as "thank you" for gifts, planning games that his friends enjoy, or choosing a menu that they like. Furthermore, in helping you get the house ready for the party, and preparing the food and the entertainment, he will begin to feel the first stirrings of pride in his home, and in inviting people to enjoy its hospitality.

Children from four to seven are at the ideal age for birthday parties. They are usually gregarious, they like games, they can appreciate entertainment, and they have mastered, or are in the process of mastering, the rudiments of respectable behavior. Parties held for two- and three-year-olds are, to be quite honest, given mainly for the mother's pleasure. She enjoys seeing her child (and the others) dressed for the occasion, surrounded by friends — the center of attraction. Whether or not it gives the child as much pleasure depends on his degree of social consciousness, his "maturity," and his friendliness. Many two-year-olds, for example, have not developed much interest in their contemporaries, and others are actually upset by being thrown in with a large group of children. They are too young to understand the significance of the occasion or their part in it. Their attention span is not capable of lasting through the activities overanxious mothers have planned. Truly, the best birthday celebration for a two-year-old, and even for many three-year-olds, is a family supper, or perhaps an hour-long "party" with one or two young guests who are neighbors or regular visitors — with whom the birthday child is completely at home. In either event, the child opens his three or four gifts first — not so many so that he is confused and cannot appreciate them. One or two favorite games are played, or his mother may read a story or show one short cartoon on a home movie projector. Then the children (or the family) sit down to a simple meal of the birthday child's favorite food. It may be (and probably is) peanut butter and jelly sandwiches and Coke, followed always by ice cream and birthday cake. Even at two, the blowing-out-the-candles ceremony is important. The child may not understand about making a wish, or what good luck is, but he *likes* to blow out candles.

Four- and five-year-olds are generally mature enough to really *enjoy* their birthdays. They love being the center of attention, they look forward to getting presents, they can participate in games or entertainment, and they will be eager to help you make the plans. Children of that age should be consulted — about *whom* they want to invite, *what* games they want to play, and *when* and *where* they would like their party to take place. Naturally, some of their ideas are bound to be totally impractical. They may want to invite the entire nursery school, or they may think an outdoor picnic in November would be just the thing.

You, the birthday child's mother, must guide, suggest, and decide, but always listen, and discuss the pros and cons of his ideas.

Even at this age, the best parties are not too big, don't last too long, and are planned so that there are no "lulls." Presents, games, entertainment, and food follow one right after the other. Here are some guidelines for you which may help in planning your child's fourth, fifth, or sixth birthday party.

1. *Limit the number of guests to eight. In that way they can all participate in planned events more or less at once, and, for example, no one child has a long wait for his turn to pin the tail on the donkey. Eight children can also be seated at a dining room table easily, and there will not be too much noise and confusion if you show movies, hire a magician, or have other entertainment.*

2. *Limit the duration of the party. Two to two and a half hours is maximum. Divide the time this way: One-half hour for guests' arrival and present-opening; one-half hour for active supervised games — races, musical chairs, a treasure hunt (very popular if treasures are not too well hidden), spider web, and so on; one-half hour to forty-five minutes for entertainment. A magician (at this age, even a very amateur magician can be*

a smash hit), movie cartoons, a clown act (juggling, for example), or even a "story hour"; one-half hour to forty-five minutes for eating and getting ready to leave.

3. Organize the two hours so that the party "moves." If you plan a "spider web" game (the child follows his own piece of string up, over, and around obstacles until he comes to a prize at the end), have it laid out before the guests arrive. Have treasure-hunt treasures already hidden. If your entertainer needs props, see that they are there when he is ready to begin. Have your movie projector threaded and ready to go. And finally, have the food laid out on trays to be brought in as soon as the children are seated.

4. Be sure that you have plenty of assistants. Supervision and organization insure the success of a party for four- or five-year-olds. Ask two or three of the children's mothers to stay and help you out. You could ask them all, but you might end up having to give the mothers more attention than you give the children.

5. Try to plan a variety of games, so that one child will not win them all. If you have nothing but races, little Paul, the athlete of the crowd, will go home with all the prizes. Your child participates, of course, but if he wins a game, the runner-up should be given the

prize. This is part of the training of a good host, and can be explained to him this way: Tell him that since he was the one to receive the presents from his friends, it is only fair that they should be the ones to receive the prizes.

6. Although time should be carefully organized, the children should also be allowed a few minutes to relax and play what they wish. The best time for this is during the first half hour, and possibly for a few minutes at the end to "blow off steam" and calm down before they go home.

7. Older children are able to cope with larger parties and longer periods of entertainment. The overall time should still not be so long that it cannot be filled with action, but the movies or the show may last an hour and the games may be more "intellectual." It has been my experience that the most successful parties for children over six are those which involve a trip to some form of entertainment, either preceded or followed by a meal at home or in a restaurant — complete, of course, with birthday cake. For boys, trips to a sports event are generally a great success. Girls, or mixed groups, can be taken to the zoo, the circus, a movie, a carnival, or an amusement park. If tickets are required, be sure to get them in advance. If you plan to do any

of these, the group must *be small, so that it can be easily supervised, and so the children will not annoy other spectators.*

8. Unless your child is celebrating his birthday with a real family party — all generations included, it is best to invite guests of approximately the same age. Six- or seven-year-olds are bored stiff with games a four-year-old can handle, and the four-year-old cannot possibly compete in the activities the seven-year-old would choose. You will have a far easier job, and the children will have much more fun, if you only ask guests who are within a year of your own child's age.

The Importance of "Thank You"

Birthday parties present one of the first and best opportunities for teaching your child to say thank you. If you have insisted that he do this every day — whenever you do something for him or give him anything special — it will come perfectly naturally to him to say thank you to his friends when they give him their presents. But many mothers are rushed or preoccupied, or lazy, or possibly just don't think it is important, so they do not bother to pursue the instruction daily. The child's lack of manners in this respect will not affect his life at home — his family will love him whether he says thank you or not. But if you want your youngster to develop the self-confidence and self-respect that other people's admiration will give him, you must teach him how to earn that admiration. The child who says thank you (and please also) naturally and warmly, has mastered the earliest lesson in manners. So do insist, before your child reaches birthday-party age, that thank you become a habit. When he is the host, stay near him as the party starts and he receives his gifts, and remind him, each time he appears to be forgetting. If your child is one of the guests, be sure that he knows he is to thank his friend *and* his friend's mother when the party is over. Don't just stay in your car, or on the steps, and wait for him to come out when you go to pick him up. Go in, thank the hostess yourself for inviting him, and make sure that he says thank you, too. It isn't stuffy, it isn't old-fashioned — it is simply a start in teaching your youngster the importance of courtesy and appreciation.

Birthdays may also provide the first opportunity for you to tell him about thank-you notes. He should learn that thank-yous cannot be forgotten simply because the person who sends a gift is not there. When he is very little, you must, of course, write his thank-you notes for him. But even at two or three you can help him to make a mark representing his signature. Don't ever let him think that it is you who will say thank you *for* him. Give him the idea that you are doing it to-gether — that you are just helping him out. As soon as he can write at all, he should write his own notes. Help him with the wording, spelling, or whatever he asks you. But let him *do* it (except the address!) and his grandmother or his godparents will be just de-lighted with his efforts.

In the Supermarket

My daughter-in-law said to me a couple of months after her son was born, "Can you imagine, before Casey was born, I was so worried about taking him to market — I was afraid he would cry and people would think he was a cranky baby or I was a bad mother!"

In one sentence, she put her finger on the precise reason that children *do* behave badly in supermarkets and other stores. Their parents are *afraid* of exerting discipline for fear that the youngster will raise a fuss.

My daughter-in-law soon found that the baby was fine in the market — he enjoyed being wheeled around in the cart and having older ladies gurgle at him and admire him. She also realized that if he was tired and cried a bit, no one really paid any attention.

When your youngster outgrows the cart or his stroller, of course, it is not so simple. The best possible approach is to tell him beforehand what you do or do not expect him to do. When he is very small, you can insist that he stay beside you, holding onto the cart — "helping" you to push it. As he gets a little older and wants to explore on his own, he should be told to stay near enough so that you can see him, or find him quickly. *Before* you go into the store tell him that he must decide whether he would prefer to behave himself while you are shopping, or to stay in the car. If the car is locked, the keys removed, the brake on firmly, and the car in gear, there is no reason he should not be left there. If he chooses to go in, as he undoubtedly will, you must stick to your ultimatum. If he starts to run about, knock things off shelves, or misbehave in any way, take him firmly by the hand — without scolding or yelling at him — and put him into the car. Remind him of the choice you gave him. Tell him that he may have the same choice again the next time you shop, and if he does not live up to your expectations, the result will be the same. Marketing would be a great deal easier for all of us if more mothers would follow this course.

If you do not have a car, the only alternative is to be firm and refuse to allow him to run loose. You probably will draw some critical looks if he has a temper tantrum, but if you keep your cool temper, and hold on to him quietly until he agrees to walk with you, it will pay off on future trips.

For the sake of your neighbors and fellow shoppers, do not allow your child to use a cart as a racing vehicle. This generally happens when you have two or three children with you, and it becomes a menace to everyone in the store. It may keep the youngsters "out of your hair" for a few minutes, but it is unfair to other shoppers. Furthermore, the children are developing a total disregard for people and property.

Another trap which is very easy to fall into is that of giving in to your child's demand for candy or other food — on the spot. If you have no objections to his having a lollipop or whatever, at the moment, fine, but if it is just before lunch, or there are good and sufficient reasons that he should not have it, stand firm. I have seen innumerable mothers say, "No, Jimmy, not now," and then gradually weaken as Jimmy's demand turns from a request to a whine to a scream. Mother looks nervously around to see if other people are watching, and then says, "All right, just this once." Obviously, Jimmy has won the contest, and knows that he can put one over on Mother any time he has an audience. Either take Jimmy to the car at once, or pay no attention to his tantrum. Don't give him the satisfaction of seeing that he can upset you so easily.

In order to stimulate his cooperation on future trips, there is no reason you should not, occasionally, treat him to some gum or candy bought as you check out. This should be treated as a reward for especially good behavior, and it should come as a surprise. There should be no hint of bribery, no "If you're good today, Sammy, you'll get a piece of gum."

Children must learn from the very beginning that every item taken from the store has to be paid for. If you do not make this clear to three-year-old Hank, how is he to know that taking a pack of gum off the stand and putting it in his pocket is stealing? When he first does this, simply put the item back if you do not wish him to have it, and explain why. If it is something he may have, ask him to put it in the basket, and tell him you will pay for it and give it to him after you have checked out. If he continues to "help himself" as he gets older, you must take further action. You should go into the rights and wrongs of stealing more deeply with him, discussing it in relation to older people as well as children. When you catch him trying to get away with a package of candy or cookies, make him pay for it in some way. If he is old enough to have an allowance, and has change with him, make him go through the line and pay for it himself. If he has no money, pay for it yourself and take the amount out of his next allowance. If he is too young for that, make him return the article to the shelf. If he has already opened it, you must pay for it, of course, but you can explain to him that this is something he may not do, and if he does it again, he will have to stay in the car.

Climbing on the check-out counter bars or on the carts, knocking things off the shelves, moving items from one place to another, and blocking aisles are all habits which annoy other customers and make shopping more time-consuming and more of a chore. They also cost the store a considerable amount of money in wasted time on the part of employees, expenses in damaged boxes or broken jars, and repairs to store property. For your own sake (and marketing *can* be a pleasure for you, too) don't let the store become a playground. Children can and should be taught that simple fact. They will also be learning a valuable lesson in consideration for people and respect for property.

As soon as your youngster is old enough to be trusted

to leave your side, ask him to help you shop. This will give him something to do and keep him out of trouble. Even a very small child recognizes his favorite brands of cereals, drinks, and so on, and he will enjoy making selections. You must limit him, of course — send him to find *one* jar of jelly, or *two* boxes of cereal, and so on. When he is a little older and starting to learn arithmetic, make a game out of how much he can spend. Show him the prices marked on the articles and explain how they tell whether you get one can for twenty-three cents or two cans for forty-five cents. Encourage him to help you save money, but he must also learn that you prefer certain things that are more expensive because they are of higher quality. This need not, and should not, be pursued beyond the simplest explanations, but he will have fun trying to help you out, and he will be learning a little about discrimination and the value of money at the same time. This will, of course, take some extra time, so try to plan your day to allow for it.

On Public Transportation

Bus, subway, and train trips are exciting, pleasurable events in the lives of small children. But unless the mothers of those children impose certain restrictions on them, the ride can be anything but pleasurable for other passengers. These trips also provide parents with an excellent opportunity to teach their children more about thoughtfulness, and becoming a cooperative member of society. Some of the suggestions which follow might serve as a lesson for many adults, too!

Many people seem to feel that because they pay for transportation, they have a right to deface the equipment, to steal anything removable, to litter, and, in general, to act as they would not think of doing at home or in any private car or facility. Furthermore, they permit their children to behave in the same way. You surely do not want your child to become a destructive, obnoxious traveler. Therefore it is up to *you* to teach him that public transportation facilities are entitled to the same care and respect as any others — that fellow passengers merit the same courtesy as acquaintances. To do this, you must set the example yourself, as well as exercising firm control over your youngster until considerate behavior comes to him naturally.

New York City, at one time, had a sign on its subways, "Young enough to ride for free — small enough to sit on your knee." This is directed to the mother, of course, but it is the first lesson in not taking more than one's share of space. On short rides, you, as a thoughtful mother, will not usurp an extra seat for your baby or toddler, who is just as happy on your lap. (On a longer train or plane trip, when he will get restless, and you will get tired, you are naturally entitled to a seat for him.) If you observe that slogan yourself, it will make it easier to convince him later on that he and his companions should not take up any more room than necessary. Youngsters have a tendency to take over a group of seats which is often more space than they need, thereby depriving other passengers of accommodation. Start your youngster out right, by your own example.

A friend recently told me that she had been riding on the subway, and was watching two youngsters who had been to a hardware store to buy spray paint for a project they were engaged in. One asked the other about the color he had chosen. The second boy tried to describe it, but quickly gave up. He pulled the can of paint out of the bag, and sprayed it all over the wall behind him. "There," he said, "I told you it was a sort of yellow!"

This wasn't done maliciously. The boy simply wanted to make his point, and he had never been taught respect for public property. This sort of behavior is inexcusable. It costs transportation companies millions of dollars, simply through lack of thoughtfulness on the part of the parents. If you care enough about your home and your possessions to teach your child how to treat them, follow through and see that he applies the same lessons to public buildings or equipment of any sort. These facilities are for the use of the general public, and your child should learn that on that public lies the responsibility for keeping them clean and in good repair.

Standing in line for tickets, or at the bus stop, provides another valuable "classroom." Don't let your youngster worm his way ahead. Some adults may smile indulgently as a tiny child pops up in front of them, but if that child is allowed to get away with it when he is two, it will become a habit by the time he is three. And when he is no longer such an engaging toddler, the reaction of the people in line will be less tolerant. To be fair to your youngster, make him wait in line

— with you — just as he must learn to take turns with his friends at home.

Passengers on trains, or on long bus trips, often want to sleep, to read, or to work. They are entitled to do so without being disturbed by loud voices or restless moving about. On short trips you can entertain your child by talking about the scenes you are passing, telling him stories, or playing simple word games. On longer trips, be sure you have books or crayons or any of the games devised for young travelers, to keep him busy. If your child is very young, take along a baby pillow, his favorite blanket and toy — anything that will make him comfortable and encourage him to sleep. And above all, don't fall asleep yourself — until he does!

At the Doctor's

There are very few children, I am sure, who are happy about a trip to their doctor. No matter how gentle and kind he may be, the pediatrician must give shots, or perform other procedures which hurt.

Some children start to cry the minute the car stops

at the doctor's door. Others make it through until they see the needle, and still others are brave enough or proud enough to endure the visit without a whimper. As soon as your child is old enough to understand, you can help him to be a member of the third category.

First, *never* lie to him about what the doctor is going to do. Don't tell him there will be no shot if a shot is due. Don't tell him it "won't hurt" if it will. Instead, emphasize that it will only last a second or two, and remind him of the lollipop the doctor (or you) will give him when it is over. Above all, let him know that you expect him to be brave. Don't put the thought of crying into his head by suggestion. If you tell him not to cry, he will know that is what you expect him to do.

It cannot help but upset him when he hears another child screaming in the inner office while he is in the waiting room. Play it down as much as possible and appeal to his pride. Say, "That little girl must be getting a shot, but it doesn't hurt *that* much. I guess she's just not very brave." Then, distract him as much as possible. Even though there are innumerable toys in the waiting room, take a favorite book or toy of his own with you. The others may be all in use, or they may not appeal to him if he is in a state of apprehension. He will feel more comfortable and at ease with a familiar object from home.

Because the children in the doctor's waiting room are apt to be tense and nervous, there may be more altercations than normally. If you see one building up, don't let it get out of hand. Find something to divert your youngster and remove him from the trouble spot. Do your very best to control your own annoyance — no matter who is at fault.

Above all, if you are nervous yourself, don't let your child see it. Your composure and your outward lack of worry about the visit will do more to reassure and calm him than all the words in the world.

8

Encouragement
and Development

I<small>N THE FIRST CHAPTER OF THIS BOOK</small>, I discussed some questions that all prospective parents should ask themselves — and each other. The last one, "How can we help him?" is the real subject of this chapter. The very best way we can help him is with constant encouragement. No other tactic — pleading, scorn, punishment for failure, promises, rewards — can achieve the result that comes through your praise and pleasure in your child's accomplishment. Everyone *wants*, basically, to please, but that desire can be lost or destroyed completely by lack of response or by discouragement.

There are any number of ways of encouraging your child, and because they involve thoughtfulness, and deep concern for the progress and accomplishment of another individual, they are closely related to etiquette. Encouragement goes far beyond the obvious meaning of showing your child how to do something and stimulating him to want to try it. It is actually more important in a subtler way. Your thanks, your pleasure when he does something for you, encourage him to want to do you a favor again. Your pride in a drawing for which he has been given a gold star in kindergarten, and your tone when you tell Daddy about it when he gets home encourage your youngster to try harder still, as well as stimulating his interest in drawing. Your appreciation of a pretty shell he has found on the beach adds to his pleasure in collecting. Your delight when he masters a new accomplishment — "Mommy, I tied my shoes all by myself!" — provides him with the stimulus to go on to further efforts. In short, expressing thanks and showing appreciation, both of which come naturally to a well-mannered, considerate person, serve to encourage his development as well as to teach him a lesson — by example — in human relationships.

Speaking of relationships brings up another side of your youngster's development — that of learning to relate to himself, to things, and to other people. The first is achieved partially by gaining self-confidence and self-respect as he matures. Your encouragement and praise are the prime factors in giving him that self-confidence. If he knows, because you tell him so, and he trusts you, that he is doing the right thing, he will develop the moral strength to understand criticism as well as gaining self-respect and self-assurance.

Relating to things or objects is largely a matter of recognition of the responsibilities imposed by possession. This was discussed fully in Chapter 4. Suffice it to repeat here that it is up to you to teach your youngster that appreciation and care of "things" are necessary characteristics of a responsible, mature person. Pride is also an important element in relating to one's possessions and is as desirable in its way as pride in self, in achievements, and in family. It can go too far, of course, if it is manifested by boasting or by smugness, but a reasonable amount of pride in possessions should be encouraged, because it, too, adds to one's self-respect.

Relating to other people is the most complicated and the most important of the three. It is the area in which etiquette plays the largest role. One cannot fit in, be accepted by, enjoy, or give pleasure to those around him if he does not consider their feelings as important as his own. This does not come naturally. It is something which must be learned by the results of his actions. With the help of his parents' teaching, and their encouragement, the child will find that treating others with consideration brings its own rewards. They will be selfish rewards in some ways — popularity, "treats" given in return for good behavior, praise from parents or teachers. But at the same time, because he sees the effect that consideration has, he will practice it more and more, until it comes naturally to him. His relationships with everyone around him will improve and because of this, his own self-respect will grow.

The Development of Good Taste

It is wise to allow a child to pursue whatever subjects interest him, even though there are many. He should, of course, be discouraged from getting into too many things at once and dropping them almost as soon as he starts. This only leads to a habit-forming record of non-accomplishment. But having a number of interests in which he develops a reasonable degree of understanding is of inestimable value.

Appreciation of excellence is one definition of good taste. Discrimination is another. Power to appreciate the work of other people and to discriminate between the good and the bad is a real talent in itself. In addition to the pleasure in, for example, music or art, that appreciation brings, it also leads to rewarding friendships with other people who share the same tastes.

There cannot be very many children in the world

who do not have a latent talent of some sort. One of the most rewarding things that can happen to a parent is to discover that talent in his child, and to help him develop it.

Too many mothers and fathers are inclined to try to look for a talent that *they* would like to see in their offspring. This is entirely different from discovering and encouraging the child's own interests or capabilities. A child who loves to work with his hands should not be pushed into singing lessons, simply because his parents love music. However, this does not mean that they should not try to develop his *appreciation* of music, whether or not he can play or sing a note. The more subjects a person can understand, appreciate, and enjoy, the happier and more interesting that person will be. Furthermore, if a child develops "taste" (or even skill) in one or two fields, he will be more readily able to apply the same criteria in new areas as his interests expand.

Music

Appreciation of music in general is developed best by plenty of exposure. If you are a rock fan or an admirer of country music, your child will have a tendency to enjoy that, too, since it is what he will hear most often. But a wise mother will attempt to have her child hear a variety of music. She will, for example, choose quieter records, or radio stations which play softer music at mealtime and bedtime. Listening to music frequently cannot fail to develop discrimination of some sort. You can *influence* his taste by presenting him with the best possible selections, but you cannot *force* him to like Bach better than Belafonte.

If he shows an inclination to sing or to play an instrument, by all means encourage him. Those are skills he will enjoy all his life. Never nip his enthusiasm in the bud by calling his effort "that awful noise." You have every right to restrict his playing to hours and places where he will not disturb you or anyone else, but don't limit it so much that he gives up.

When your daughter shows an honest eagerness to

learn to play the piano at six or seven years of age, let us say, ask her if she would like to take lessons. You should make it clear, however, that you will expect her to practice a certain amount and that studying music is a serious business. If she is not sure she will want to do that, the lessons should not start, and if she falters after beginning, the sessions should be canceled immediately. It is not fair to you to pay the fee for lessons that do not mean enough to her, nor is it right to push her when she finds it more of a task than she had expected. Countless youngsters have ended up by being bored with, or actually disliking music because they were forced to continue playing after they discovered it was not what they hoped for.

Drawing

An ability to draw or paint provides a tremendous amount of satisfaction. It also has some valuable side effects. A child who has been encouraged to draw from the earliest possible age may develop a most practical talent later. He may use the skill for taking notes in school, for illustrating details in many situations, and as an aid to memory. One who has recorded a fact or figure by illustration rarely forgets that information. Drawing is also an important aid in physical development. The child learns to coordinate his hand and his eye, and drawing gives him an idea about the interrelation of objects and perspective. It encourages him to really *look* at objects and study them, rather than merely seeing them and passing on.

There are a number of ways of stimulating a child's interest in this talent. I had an uncle who lived on a farm, and when I was very little, living on a farm was what I wanted most of all to do. When he came to visit, he would sit down with me and draw simple sketches of the house, the woods, the animals, and people doing farm chores. Then he would ask me to draw a picture of what I would like *my* farm to be. I'm sure his artwork was not very good but I was enchanted, and I believe it was the start of my own interest in art.

Another drawing game that children enjoy is to draw an object and ask the child what it is. If he guesses, it is his turn to draw something, and your turn to guess. Or, you can award a point for each drawing that is good enough to be identified on the first guess.

Special events can provide subjects for developing a skill in illustrating, too. With your youngster, think of something you did together during the past week. Take turns making it into a picture.. Let us take, as an example, a trip to the park. Ask him if he remembers the balloon man and suggest that he draw the balloons. Then it is his turn to pick a subject for you. "Do you remember the seals getting their dinner, Mommy?" Your seals may not be a work of art but he will admire your efforts, and this game is also excellent for memory training.

When your youngster proudly brings you a "drawing" he has made, and all you can see is a mishmash of blots and scratches, *don't* say, "That's fine, Helen. What is it?" It *can't* be fine if you don't know what it is, although to Helen it's as clear as a bell. Say, instead, "That's lovely, Helen. Tell me about it," or "Describe it to me." As her drawing improves, don't hesitate to say, "That's much better than the one you did yesterday." Your interest in each effort and your recognition of her progress will keep Helen's enthusiasm alive, and will stimulate her to try more and more advanced subjects and techniques.

Sometimes, if your child's work of art is so poor that you can think of nothing good to say about it, it is best to play a delaying action. Tell her, "It's late now and the light isn't so good," or, "I'm in the middle of getting dinner, so let's look at it in the morning." By then you will have had time to think of a way of offering constructive criticism without seeming too "down" on her effort. She, in turn, will have gotten over the first enthusiastic flush of creativity and will see her picture more clearly. She *may* not even want to show it to you the next day! In any case, no matter how disastrous an effort it is, be sure to temper your criticism with a complimentary word. You can always find something kind to say — an "interesting" line or a pretty spot of color, perhaps. Whatever it may be, emphasize it, but be sure that what you say is true.

Manual Dexterity

The degree of dexterity with which children are born varies tremendously. But fortunately, it is an asset which can be developed if encouraged. Small children should be urged to use their hands in every possible way. Cutting out paper dolls or shapes, finger-painting, drawing, buttoning and unbuttoning, tying bows and knots, pasting, building with blocks and construction toys are all excellent training. Simple carpentry work is, too, and should not necessarily be reserved for boys. In today's world, women have to do many chores formerly considered "men's work" and fathers should take pains to teach their daughters as well as their sons the elementary skills of carpentry. Hammering nails, tightening screws, using pliers, and so on, are fine training.

Young children love to "help." Let them! It may take you three times as long to accomplish your task, but it is well worth it. If your three-year-old wants to help you put away the groceries, don't turn her down because she may drop the eggs or the milk. She cannot learn how to handle things carefully if she is not allowed to try. Don't even say, "I'll take the eggs, Susie; you might drop them." This shows your lack of confidence in her, and therefore discourages her from wanting to try. You can certainly try to put the eggs into the refrigerator yourself before Susie gets ahold of them, but if she gets them first, don't take them away from her. Show her a better way to hold the box, if necessary, and praise her when she completes her chore successfully.

Get your husband's cooperation in doing the same thing with your son when he is in his workshop or working on the car.

There are children who never do develop a great deal of manual dexterity — there are others who never become good students or great athletes. These youngsters should be encouraged to concentrate on the skills they *do* have. If your child simply is not a fast runner, don't push him into trying out for the soccer team. He won't make it, and you will have increased his chances of developing an inferiority complex. Instead, search for what he *can* do well and urge him in that direction.

Collecting

Every child, I believe, goes through a period of collecting, and it is a very worthwhile interest. It is probably one of the best lessons he can have in discrimination. In the beginning the young collector will amass *everything* he can find in his chosen subject. If it is shells, he will pick up *all* the scallop shells he can find on the beach. If it is pictures of kittens he will cut out every kitten picture he can find in every magazine. Sheer quantity is his goal and you may go berserk with the shells filling every possible receptacle, or finding holes cut out of the magazine articles you had looked forward to reading. At this point, it is time for a lesson in discrimination. Don't discourage him or deride his collection, but convince him of how much more interesting it would be if he discarded duplicates and kept only the best shells or the cutest pictures. Help him select, if he will let you, because this gives you an opportunity to encourage good taste.

Your youngster's collections also give you a chance to emphasize care of property and respect for it. If you treat his shells as objects of value he will appreciate more readily the things that mean something to you — and others. In teaching him how to take care of his treasures he will absorb a lesson in taking care of property in general — even that which he cares less about.

Collections can be a great source of pride. They may, in much the same way as a child's unusual phrase or funny expression, become part of family lore.

In our summer home we have a framed case of carefully lacquered, mounted scallop shells of beautiful color and design, made by one of our sons when he was six or seven. They have made a fine contribution to family pride and to his own self-esteem for many years.

Intrafamily Relationship

Several pages back, I mentioned that relating to other people is the most complicated and the most important of the relationships a child must develop. Since the members of his family will be the first "other people" he will be exposed to, his method of relating to others will start with them. This will begin, of course, the day he is born and the first person he will relate to will be his mother. But very rapidly, his father, brothers, and sisters, and anyone else who is constantly around will enter his range of consciousness. He will learn, very early, that he can affect their actions or reactions by his own behavior, and that their behavior can affect him. He will establish his own place in the family relationship, and for a time it will be static. But circumstances change. Other children are born, someone dies, the family breaks up, or all or some members move. Each situation changes the way in which the members relate to each other.

The only way parents can prepare children for the changes and the varying situations which will face them is to give them a solid basis for maintaining a happy relationship with everyone. And the *most* solid basis anyone can develop in establishing a relationship of any sort — with older people, younger people, or his own contemporaries — is consideration. If a child is taught to think of other people first from the time he is very small he will be able to successfully establish his place, first in his family, and later in the community. Whether he is an only child, or one of ten, he must learn how to relate to his parents and/or his brothers and sisters successfully. The relationship he develops with them will set the pattern for his relationship with the rest of the world, so don't wait. Start teaching him consideration, through example first, and instruction later, from the day he is born.

The only child

All first babies are, of course, "only children" to begin with. They have no competitors for the attention and affection of their parents, and as long as no second children arrive, their position is secure. The greatest danger is that they will receive so much attention, and find that family life revolves around them so completely, that they will have a very difficult time adjusting to changing circumstances. When the changes occur, as they do when another child arrives, the situation may be traumatic for a time, but the natural spreading of affection and care is healthy. The first child, if he receives encouragement and understanding, eventually learns to accept his new position in the family.

The baby who remains an only child, while he still has the benefits of undivided love and attention, is actually in a far more difficult position. His parents, no matter how they may try, cannot make up for other youngsters in the family. He cannot compete with them, play with them, fight with them or have the same feelings for them as he would a near contemporary. Therefore, if you are the parents of an only child, don't try to "make up to him" for his loneliness by being brother and sister to him. Maintain the same parent-child relationship that you would if there were more children. The most important thing you *can* do is to see that he is with other children as much as he possibly can be. Since there are none in his family, he must learn about fitting in with and getting along with his peers on the outside. He is a little person in a big people's world at home, and he should have the experience of being with others his size whenever he can. It is only competition with other children and the challenge of "I can do that, too" which will make him develop normally, and keep him from becoming introverted and insecure when he reaches school age. Nursery school is almost a "must" for an only child — to give him the feeling of belonging to a group.

Mothers of a single child also tend to be very overprotective. He is their one and only, and they could not bear to have anything happen to him. So, he is not allowed to grow up, is inclined to be overly "coddled," and often becomes a "sissy." It is only fair to him for his mother to untie those apron strings. She may feel that she is deserting him, being cruel, and so on, but for his sake, withdrawing from him and forcing him to stand on his own two feet is the only way she can encourage him to be self-reliant and independent.

The second child arrives

The first child, as mentioned above, has few problems when he is still the only child. But consider what happens to him when a second child arrives. His world is literally turned upside down. A new baby demands a tremendous amount of his mother's time — time that used to be entirely his. Her attention, too, is now focussed on the new arrival. There are often physical effects. He may be moved to another room or forced to share his room with the baby. His mealtimes may change, or he may be left to feed himself while mother nurses or feeds the baby. Perhaps she cannot go for walks with him because it is too cold for the baby outside, and he cannot be left alone. And so on and on. Is it any wonder that there is very apt to be a strong antipathy between the first and second child?

You, as a parent, can do much to improve the relationship. First, you can include the older child in all your plans and preparations for the coming arrival. You can build up his confidence by making him feel necessary to you — what a help he will be with the baby! Once the new baby arrives you can carry this through insofar as possible. Don't make the mistake of constantly saying, "Don't touch the baby, your hands are dirty," "Stop talking, you'll wake the baby up," "Leave me alone, can't you see I'm feeding the baby?" You cannot, of course, allow him to hurt the baby with roughness or carelessness, but you can be sure that he knows and understands just what *is* good or bad for the baby. If his efforts are simply misguided rather than malicious, correct him and let him touch, hold, and play with his brother or sister as much as you possibly can — it is the best way to develop love and protectiveness as opposed to jealousy and resentment.

The older child should be given a large extra dose of affection at this time. He *is* insecure and he needs reassurance badly. His parents should spend extra time with him when the baby has been put to bed or is napping, so that he will have their undivided attention. He should be given some special treats which the baby cannot have, or occasionally taken on outings where the baby cannot go. In short, he must be made to feel that he is still an individual, and as important as ever in his parents' eyes.

The second child is born into an entirely different set of circumstances, which can be equally difficult. He never has the advantage that the first child had — that of simply *being* the first. No matter how much parents may love all their children, there can never be another occasion quite like the birth of the oldest. When the younger arrives, he gets the lion's share, but not *all*, of his mother's attention. His older brother or sister is there from the beginning so the baby has no readjustment problem, but he is faced with a competitive goad right at the start. Very early in his life, for example, a little boy wants to be able to do what his big brother can do, and of course, he cannot. So there is frustration, and there is challenge almost at once. Different children react in different ways. Some develop slavish devotion and admiration for the older child and attempt to emulate him in every way. Others are jealous, hate their sibling, or give up the fight and withdraw. The wise mother encourages the admiration, but does not urge the younger child to develop in the same way or to compete. She searches for his particular talents, and stimulates an interest in those activities in which he will excel. She discourages jealousy and envy in the same way — by giving the younger child self-respect and confidence in his own abilities. In a large family it is unusual to see first and second children who are very similar or very close to each other. When there are three or more in the family, it is more common for the first and third or second and fourth to be alike and to be friendly, as they are not so close in age and size and therefore there is less rivalry.

First children find different ways to try to ward off the threat that they feel the new baby imposes. Some become aggressive and "show-offy," to draw attention to themselves. Others resort to being naughty — to deliberate disobedience or destruction, for the same purpose. Still others, seeing the attention that the little one is getting, revert to babyhood themselves. They may start wetting themselves again, return to baby talk, or demand a bottle.

Parents are often confused and very upset by these

reactions. They should not be, because such reactions are natural and explicable. In general these symptoms should be treated as minor upsets, and there should be few recriminations and no retaliation. The child who is being destructive or disobedient must be restrained, naturally, but it is the cause rather than the result which must be tackled. Punishment will not cure it — punishment will only cause additional resentment. The answer lies in convincing the child that he has not been replaced — he is still loved and admired. He should also be made to see that he has great advantages — he can do so many things the baby cannot do. When he realizes this, and that his position in his parents' affection is not threatened, devotion to and pride in his younger brother or sister will start to develop.

The adopted child

In spite of all that has been written and recommended on the subject, there are still parents who do not want to tell their child he is adopted. They think, in spite of all odds, that they can keep the secret from him forever. They feel that the child will not have the same love for them that he would for his "real" parents.

They are wrong. The "secret" of the adoption is impossible to keep unless you choose to move to another country, sever all ties, and start a new life. Otherwise, several people *must* know about it, and if several do, more will eventually. How much crueler for the child to learn of his adoption through a chance remark, or because a playmate teases him about it, than to have it properly presented to him by his parents!

The fact of being adopted is nothing to be ashamed of — it should be treated as something to be proud of. When your child is old enough to understand at all — at two or three, perhaps — start to mention it occasionally, as something very special. "*You* are our *adopted* son — we chose you over all the other babies in the world." Use the word "adopted" naturally and frequently so that he will know there is nothing undesirable or furtive about it. Then if, as sometimes happens, a young friend says, "You don't belong to your mommy and daddy — you're adopted," he will be forewarned and that is to be forearmed. He may be somewhat upset, but you have already provided him with a rebuttal, and all you need to do is repeat it — "We *chose* you because we loved you best. . . ."

When he is older he may question your love for him when he discovers that he is not a "blood" relative. Again, you have a perfect ready-made argument. "Daddy and I are not related by blood either and you know how much we love each other. We love you the same way — the 'blood' doesn't matter at all." As far as his love for you — he will, like any child, love you because you are the only parents he knows. Just as a natural child would, he will have his ups and downs — his moments of anger, suspicion, resentment, and so on — but if you have treated him as you would your own child, he will react in exactly the same way, and give you the same love and respect he would have given his "real" parents.

A child who is adopted as a baby should be treated as your own in every way. There is never any question about what he calls you — you *are* Mom and Dad to him. He undoubtedly will, at some point, develop a curiosity about his own parents. Satisfy him as much as you can, but don't dwell on it, or let him do so. If you adopted him through an agency, you will not know a great deal in any case, as they make very sure that identities remain hidden. If your child knows that there is no way of finding his real parents, and is secure and happy with you, this urge to look into his past will quickly subside.

If you knew your child's parents, even though he was tiny when they died, you should tell him everything you possibly can about them. They are dead, and he will accept the fact that he can never know them, but he will feel more confidence in you if he knows that you are not trying to hide anything. He is also entitled to the knowledge, and whatever pleasure or pride it may bring him.

The situation is rather different if you adopt a child who is old enough to have known and loved his own parents. He may, for example, resent you very much. He probably will feel very bitter about having lost his mother and father and will not wish to, or be able to, transfer his affections for some time. He may feel that you are trying to "force" him, or that you are trying to replace his parents. Don't do either — let nature take its course. Trite as it sounds, time does heal wounds, and if you wait for him to come to you, he *will* eventually turn to you for the consolation he needs.

Don't insist that a child in these circumstances call you by the same names he used for his mother and father. This is one situation when the use of first names may provide an answer. Possibly you and the youngster can find nicknames acceptable to you both, or, if he is already fond of you, another derivative of mother or father will do. "Aunt" and "Uncle" are other possibilities.

Give him all the love and sympathy you can, without seeming unnatural. It is most important to him that his life return to normal, and the more you can do as an ordinary parent would, the quicker his re-adjustment will take place. Talk about his parents whenever he wishes to, but avoid any criticism or implication that he is better off now. Encourage him to be proud of his background, and to honor the memory of his parents. If you are honest in this, and treat him just as you would (or do, if you have other children) your own child, he will soon accept you happily as an addition to, not a replacement of, his own mother and father.

From Can't to Can

Children have a very real fear of their own lack of ability. They are very inclined to refuse a challenge if there is a chance they cannot meet it. Adults are able to judge whether something is within their capabilities or not — children do not have the experience to know. This insecurity can be overcome to a large extent by your display of confidence in your child, and your encouragement. However, you would be making a mistake if you were not honest — if you encouraged him to try something you knew he could not succeed in. In fiction, the little crippled girl may grow up to be a famous dancer, or the Ugly Duckling may grow into a Swan. In real life it rarely happens. The little girl and her parents, if they have good sense, will look for something she *can* do well — without the suffering and probably disappointments a dancing career would offer.

Occasionally a child's timidity, or lack of confidence in being able to do something, is the result of a bad experience. Perhaps he fell into a swimming pool before he knew how to swim, so he is scared to death of the water. Or he was bitten by a dog when he was very small, and has been terrified of animals ever since.

It is far more likely, however, that fears such as these are instilled by thoughtless parents. The mother who shrieks, "Henry, come back, don't go so near the edge of the pool," is inadvertently convincing Henry that water is dangerous, something to be avoided. It may be years before he can control this fear and feel any pleasure — or confidence — in swimming. Similarly, the mother who is always saying, "Susie, don't go near that dog — he may bite," is instilling a fear of animals and depriving Susie of the joy that can come from confidence in, and love of pets.

Children know that there are many things they cannot do — they see evidence of it every day. Therefore parents must be careful not to discourage in order to avoid the development of an "I can't" syndrome. Of course there are children who are smart enough to take advantage of "I can't," too. Our daughter, the some-times-victim of two older brothers, used it frequently. When they tried to order her around, to fetch and carry for them, she would simply say, "No, I can't, I'm too little."

In general, however, the child who constantly whines "I can't" lacks self-confidence. It is up to his parents to change this to "I can." The youngster's environment can affect him severely. For instance, if he grows up in a city, he must, when he is small, be put in a carriage or held by the hand when he goes for a walk. He may soon lose all sense of independence and it is up to his parents to counteract this by finding other safer areas in which he may do things entirely on his own.

That brings up one of the few dangers of too much encouragement. Possibly it can also create too much dependence. But this is not hard to avoid. If you can make yourself say, "This is the way to do it, Johnny — now you do it yourself," and then leave him alone to try, you will be combining encouragement and independence successfully. Done in this way, it can *never* be too much, so don't hold back. The greatest gift you can give your child is self-confidence — the firm belief that whatever he wants to do, he *can*.

9

The Beauty of Truth

I f ONE LIVED strictly according to the basic code of etiquette — that is, always practicing consideration, unselfishness, and kindness, he would, inevitably, be an admirable person. Presumably he could not achieve that status without also being honest because, on the face of it, dishonesty always affects someone adversely. Therefore, truth, the root of honesty, is an essential part of etiquette. And yet, is it *always* kind to tell the truth? It is not, and the *truly* admirable person recognizes that, and knows where to draw the line.

To train a child to be truthful, and at the same time teach him to be tactful, is possibly one of the most important challenges a mother must face. It is further complicated by the necessity of teaching him the difference between fact and fiction.

Let's Pretend

Every mother — at least every mother with a sense of humor and common sense — frequently plays some form of "Let's pretend" with her child. She takes an imaginary bite of food to keep him company as he eats dinner, she plays "horse" or "engine" as she gives him a piggyback ride, or pretends any number of imaginative things to make him laugh and stimulate his inventiveness. Most children have little trouble in differentiating between this "play world" and the real world, although it is wise to emphasize the dividing line by saying, "Time to get down off this horse now and come in to supper."

You will surely want to allow your child to give free range to his imagination, but at the same time you must teach him the importance of knowing it *is* fancy and not fact. The following story illustrates how confused a child may become, and at the same time, what a thoughtful mother can do to help.

Five-year-old Jimmy had gotten into the habit of exaggerating or telling outright untruths so regularly that no one believed a word he said. He was becoming emotionally upset, because for a time people questioned every statement he made, and later they became so annoyed with his answers that they ignored him entirely.

His mother became more and more concerned but could not seem to convince him that once a person begins to lie, his words have less and less value, and finally people neither like him nor listen to him. One day she picked up a newspaper, and to illustrate the importance of truth, she told him how essential it was for a reporter to be completely honest and accurate, because his reports were read by so many people and could have so much effect on the way they thought and acted. Jimmy understood, but asked what the reporter would do if he just wrote down ideas that came into his head, and they turned out to be untrue. His mother realized that she found the key — Jimmy simply didn't *know* the difference between truth and make-believe. She explained that stories, novels, and fairy tales are fiction because someone has "made them up."

"Then stories are not lies?" asked Jimmy.

"No," replied his mother, "not as long as they are *called* fiction and no one tries to pretend that they are true."

"Then," said Jimmy, "if I tell you something is a

story when I've made it up, and I tell you I mean it when it's real, you'll believe me?"

"Of course," answered his mother, and Jimmy's problem was solved. He had never lied deliberately — he was simply unable to separate the truth from a story.

Each year thousands of children ask, "Is there really a Santa Claus?" Some parents feel they are faced with a decision — should they stick to the literal truth and deny Saint Nick, or allow the youngster another year or two of happy dreams? Frankly, I cannot imagine depriving a child of the thrill of dreaming of Santa and his reindeer delivering gifts, and waking up to find the presents under the tree — a true miracle that took place while he slept. Nor can I imagine a child's world without Winnie-the-Pooh, Peter Rabbit, or Cinderella. It would be far more valuable for those parents who stunt their children's imaginations by exposing them only to "true" stories, to devote themselves to teaching the youngsters the wide difference between the beauty of make-believe and the ugliness of a real lie.

A related fantasy, which is especially common in an only child, is the imaginary playmate. This is not harmful in itself as long as the child knows deep down that the fantasy *is* a figment of his imagination. It is, however, wise to investigate the cause, as it may be a symptom of a more serious problem. Very often the reason for these fantasies is simply loneliness — either that of the only child, or alienation from brothers or sisters. At the time, they serve to get a child through a difficult period — until he goes to school, perhaps, or the family relationships which are troubling him are changed.

Whatever form they take, human, or perhaps animal, they are very real to the children who visualize them, and parents should not ridicule them, nor try to destroy the image. Not only will that remove what may possibly be a needed crutch, but it can dampen imagination and creativity. Almost invariably, they fade away or disappear quite suddenly — as soon as the need for them is gone. While they exist, mother should make it very clear that she accepts and recognizes the existence of the imaginary character, but *only* as fiction. She knows, and she assumes her child knows, the image is not real.

The "White Lie"

It is essential that your child learn the difference between tactful evasion (a little white lie), whose nature is courtesy or kindness, and the evasion of truth, whose motive is saving face, causing injury, or avoiding punishment. It is extremely difficult to point out to a child exactly how far he should go with the "white lie." It is all a matter of consideration — will he hurt someone's feelings if he tells the bald truth? When he is very small he should learn that he must say certain things and make certain responses even though they are not literally true. He need think no further — he simply learns to say thank you whether he likes the gift just given to him or not, or he knows he replies, "Fine, thank you" to the question "How are you?" This is not dishonesty — it is simply following a form of give-and-take which is known and accepted and therefore breaks down a barrier and smooths the way to further communication. "Thank you" is a requirement, because no matter what you think of the gift or favor you have received, it indicates appreciation of the effort.

As your child matures, however, you must go beyond teaching him what he must say, and instruct him in what *not* to say. Children are naturally forthright and honest, and without your guidance, they do not think of the effect of their words on others.

A bit of the reverse technique is helpful here. When your child has embarrassed you to death by — quite truthfully — saying, "Gee, that lady has fat legs, hasn't she?" ask him how he would feel if someone pointed at him and said, "My, that little boy looks funny with his two front teeth out." This may not be a strong enough remedy in itself, and you may have to actually make some derogatory remarks or even get someone else to do so to make your point. When he does *feel* how such remarks can hurt, he will appreciate how much kinder silence can be than truth.

You must coach a child in advance for a specific situation. For example, if your Joanie has a birthday coming soon, explain to her that she is not to say, "I hate playing with dolls" as she opens a box with a lovely baby doll inside. She need not lie. All she need do is say thank you to show appreciation for the effort made. Or, if you are taking her out to dinner, she must be taught not to say, "I hate spinach," when spinach is passed. She need not eat it, but neither should she mention it. "No, thank you" is all she should say. As she gets older, she will understand this better, especially if she has been brought up in a home where kindness and consideration are taken for granted. Until that time, it is your job to try to foresee the danger spots, and to instill in her that thoughtfulness which will make your lessons unnecessary.

The Malicious Lie

A real lie — a malicious lie — is one that has fear, meanness, or self-advancement behind it. The most common lie by far is told for fear of punishment. Fear of being punished for breaking something, for hurting someone, for stealing, or for being "found out" leads a normally honest child to try to lie his way out of the situation.

This brings up a very important point — your child should always be given the benefit of the doubt — until he is *proved* wrong. If you do not do this, you are not displaying the trust and confidence in him that he needs. If Davy claims that it was not he who cut the slice out of the pie cooling on the kitchen counter, you must believe him unless you have good reason to suspect that he is lying. If you do, of course, you must face him with the evidence, try to find out why he lied, and take whatever steps you think are necessary to prevent it from happening again. If it reoccurs frequently, some form of punishment may be in order. If it is a first offense, an open discussion may be enough.

The motive behind every malicious lie is necessarily bad — if it weren't, lying would not be necessary. But even with real lies there are degrees of seriousness, and the punishment should fit that degree. The boy who calls a tennis shot "out" when it actually touched the line is not committing a mortal sin, but he is establishing a pattern of dishonesty, and this should be made clear to him. The boy who cheats usually hurts only himself because even though he might win this particular game because of his call, he will soon find himself without friends to play with. Cheating is a form of dishonesty which generally reaps its own reward — or punishment.

The lie which is told out of revenge or hate, and causes harm to someone else, is infinitely more serious. It is also far less normal than simple "cheating" for one's own gain. If your child takes out his frustration or anger by "lying" his friends into trouble, don't let the situation develop. Take steps at once. The only cure is to get to the cause — *why* is he bitter or unhappy enough to want to cause hurt? If you cannot find out, through analysis of your own success as a mother, or by getting him to confide in you, you should consult your pediatrician and ask for his recommendation for psychiatric help.

You, as a parent, must remember that no matter

what you tell your child about honesty and dishonesty, it is your example that he will follow. There is no use in talking about the beauty of truth and the ugliness of a lie if you do not speak truthfully yourself. And yet, to teach him to shade the truth when it is for a reason of kindness or mercy, is far closer to the *spirit* of truth than to teach him to blindly stick to a truth with merciless honesty that can only hurt.

I have chosen to end this book with these words about truth (or honesty) because I believe it to be, perhaps, the most important thing you can give your child. In the first chapter I asked the question, "How can we help our child?" Teaching him to be honest, with himself and with others, is surely one of the essential lessons. If he *knows* that he is truthful, in spite of all evidence against him, and he understands the shaded areas between truth and tact, he will never lose his self-respect and he will be able to live with himself.

None of us is perfect, as I have said before. The best that parents can do is to lead their child *toward* perfection — to the best of their, and the child's, ability. In the area of truth this is quite possible. Parents' own honesty with their child will be reflected in his honesty with others. It is a goal of prime importance — one worth striving for. Whether or not your parents instilled in you a reverence for honesty, don't neglect it in bringing up your child. We are not aiming at *maintaining* a level of child-rearing, we are aiming at improving it. Whatever else you do or do not pass on to your children, *do* convince them of the beauty of truth, now that it's your turn.

Index

as aim of life, 23
as basis for human relation-
    ships, 259
of child's feelings, 51, 54,
    96
of child's relaxation, 112–
    113
within family, 28, 67, 140
for friends, 127
of meals, 175
of others, 12, 96–97, 135,
    223, 235, 247, 280–
    281, 284
and promptness, 152–153
and "thank you," 135, 280
on transportation, 237–238
value, 39, 246
"white lie" as, 279–281
    See also possessions
constructive impulse, 118
contentment, 21–22
contradiction, 194
convenience, parents': rela-
    tion to treatment of
    child, 35–37, 82–83
cooperation, 66, 98–99
courage, 23, 58
courtesy. *See* manners
creativity, 279
criticism, parents'
    avoidance of, 159
    of drawings, 253–254
    excessive, 17–18
    of friends, 124
    at meals, 163
    need for, 17
    unnecessary, 94–96
curtsying, 214

deception, parents', 53
decisions
    child's, 96

concerning conflicts, 35–37
reversing, 20
defeatist attitude, 17, 90
demands, of child
    to household help, 199
    precedence of, 35–37, 82–
        83
    treatment of, 35–36, 70,
        86–87, 134–135
demands, parents', 109–114,
    133–134
denials, 80–82, 86
dependability, parents', 53
destruction, of property, 80,
    117–120, 265
development, child's
    of interests, 248–257
    parents' role, 22–29, 246–
        248
    physical, 252, 254
diaries, child's, 106–108
disagreements, parents', over
    child, 19–20
disappointments
    in career, 270
    in child rearing, 11
discipline
    aim, 65
    in front of others, 83–85,
        212
    lack of, 75–76
    obedience, in relation to,
        65–66
    parents' agreement about,
        19–20
    parents' responsibility, 8
    relaxation of, 70–71
    self-, 65
    validity of, 79–90
    See also punishment
discrimination, 23, 66, 124,
    144, 248, 256